Testimonial Quotes

"The most clear, succinct and understandable book on memory I've ever read."

> Bill Grove, CPAE
> First President
> National Speakers Association

"Bob creates an excellent learning atmosphere: his material is very useful, lively, light-hearted and fun, with a high retention level."

> Margaret M. McDonald
> Manager, Special Events
> Marriott Corporation

"I would have said I can't remember when I've read a better memory book, but thanks to Bob, I do remember...and I haven't."

> Ron Wiggins
> Columnist
> The Palm Beach Post

"Bob shares his memory skills and techniques in a clear, concise, understandable, easy to follow manner. This is a 'must read' for anyone in sales. Everyone likes when you remember their name ——a certain way to increase your profits. Thanks, Bob."

> Rosemary "Molly" Mistal, Ph.D.
> State Director of Training
> The Prudential Florida Realty

"Mr. Burg takes a subject intimidating to many and turns it into fun!"

> Claude W. Olney, J.D.
> Author
> *Where There's a Will There's an "A"*

About National Seminars...

National Seminars Group has its finger on the pulse of America's business community. We've trained more than 2 million people in every imaginable occupation to be more productive and advance their careers. Along the way, we've learned a few things. Like what it takes to be successful ... how to build the skills to make it happen ... and how to translate learning into results. Millions of people from thousands of companies around the world turn to National Seminars for training solutions.

National Press Publications is our product and publishing division. We offer a complete line of the finest self-study and continuing-learning resources available anywhere. These products present our industry-acclaimed curriculum and training expertise in a concise, action-oriented format you can put to work right away. Packed with real-world strategies and hands-on techniques, these resources are guaranteed to help you meet the career and personal challenges you face every day.

The Memory System

Remember everything
you need when you
need it

By Bob Burg

National Press Publications

A division of Rockhurst College Continuing Education Center, Inc.
6901 West 63rd Street • P.O. Box 2949 • Shawnee Mission, KS 66201-1349
1-800-258-7246 • (913) 432-7757

The Memory System
Published by National Press Publications, Inc., January 1992
© 1992 National Press Publications, a division of Rockhurst College
Continuing Education Center, Inc.

Printed in the United States of America.

17   18   19   20

ISBN #1-55852-068-6

Acknowledgments

There are so many people I need to thank regarding this book that it would take a separate book just to list them. Instead, let me thank several groups of people. One is the National Speakers Association, more than 3,500 of the nicest, supportive, most sharing and caring people in the world (this includes my wonderful friends in the South Florida Chapter).

Those who gave me moral and written support when it was needed (which was always). Renata, I couldn't have done this without you, and had I tried, it wouldn't have come out as good. Ron, thank you. Your expert writing skills rescued my readers from many of my overused expressions and amateurish syntax. I thank my office staff, who help make my speaking habit possible by keeping me on the road constantly (come to think of it, that's probably where they like me best).

To all of you, I wish you the best of success ... "AND GOOD MEMORIES!"

Bob Burg

Dedication

Mom and Dad — Your love, support and encouragement
have kept me going for 33 years.
Words will never be able to describe what you mean to me.

To Samantha,
my beautiful 2-year-old niece and Goddaughter — I love you!

FOREWORD

Attack your lack! I've always admired any person who had the integrity to admit a shortcoming and the courage to turn that shortcoming into his or her greatest strength. That's what my friend Bob Burg has done.

His lack was the ability to remember names. He was embarrassed about it. So, he sat down and studied all the memory training systems and with superb innovation came up with a teaching system that not only helped him conquer his lack but also made him one of America's leading proponents of a system that works!

He constantly tests himself and his system. I remember one time when Bob and I were standing in the lobby of a hotel in Atlanta, Georgia during the National Speakers Association Annual Convention. He was greeting almost everyone who passed by, saying hello to this one and that one and calling them by name. I asked if he were looking for someone in particular. "No," he said. "I'm testing my memory system to recall the people I met at last year's convention." I had met many of those same people, but could only nod as they approached.

Bob Burg has done more than just write a book on memory; he lives it. You'll feel Bob's energy, enthusiasm and dedication as you read about how to remember names, faces, facts, figures—whatever you wish to commit to memory—in this book. Never again will you have to avoid someone whose name you should remember but can't. Never again will you have to resort to calling people "governor," "pal," "big guy," or something similar because you can't remember their name.

This book is in your hands because you had the integrity to admit to a lack, the same lack that Bob had when he decided to do something about it. He decided to attack his weakness and make it his greatest strength. You have made that same decision. When you complete this book, you'll be amazed not only with the prowess of your memory but also with how that will boost your self-esteem and confidence. And forever more you'll remember the name of the man who helped you overcome your lack. You'll remember Bob Burg.

Arnie Warren
President
Florida Speakers Association

CONTENTS

Chapter 1 Observation—Association—(Weird) Imagination   1
Begin By Observing   1
Next Is Association   2
Here's The Answer   3
Consider The Following...   3
But What About Those Everyday Occurrences?   4
What If We Changed The Way We Did It?   4
Last, But Not Least, Imagination   5
A Fun Way To Illustrate   5
But What's A Date?   6
We Can Picture It   6
Observation, Association, And Imagination Are Always
   Involved In Memory   7

Chapter 2 Of Chain Links And Soundalikes   9
The Chain Link Method   9
Let's Try It   9
Here's How I Would Do It   10
We're Halfway Through   11
And The Results?   12
Let's Work On Imagination Skills   13
Wild And Crazy Pictures   13
It's...Unforgettable   13
Ouch! And More   14
You Can Quiz Yourself   15
The Very Important Soundalike—For Picturing The Intangible   15

Contents

A Closer Look At The Soundalike   16
Let's Do It Together   16
Five Down—Five To Go   17
Got The Hang Of It?   18
How Did You Do?   20

Chapter 3 TAKE A BREAK! Test Yourself On Memorabilia   21

Chapter 4 Remember People's Names And Faces   25
You Can Do It, Too   26
Gee, I Remember Your Face, But...   26
Attack Them One-By-One   27
The Face Is Very Important   27
Make Sure To Get The Name   28
Handling The Name Part   29
Now Lock It In   30
Let's Walk Through Two Examples   31
Continuing On, Without Even Any Pictures   32
I Bet You Remember Them   35
Just Like Learning How To Drive A Car   36
First Names Are Even Easier   36
Let's Meet Some Real Folks   39
Were You Wondering...?   41
Take These Techniques To Heart   42
First The Face...   43
Then The Name   43
Slowly Bring Them Together   44
Enhance Your Networking   44
Two Final Quick Points   45
Quick Reference—First Name Soundalikes   47
Quick Reference—Last Name Soundalikes   48

Chapter 5 English Vocabulary   63

Chapter 6 Foreign Language Vocabulary   73

**Chapter 7 Remember Numbers Via The
                  Mnemonic Alphabet   81**
Please Don't Be Intimidated   81
We Must Be Able To Picture Them   82
Here's How We Do It   83
Easy Ways To Remember The Rest   84
The Sounds Are The Key   86
A Worthwhile Exercise   87

Contents

Good For You   88
All Right, If You Insist   89
Let's Bring It Together   89
How About Another?   90
Do They All Fit?   90

Chapter 8 Mental Hooks   93
What Would It Be Worth To You?   93
Why These Particular Pictures?   96
A Quick Review   99
This Will Seem Amazing!   101
Let's Put It To The Test   104
It Isn't Even Difficult   106
Fun And Simple Drills   107
Just A Bit Of Work Will Be Greatly Rewarded   107

Chapter 9 Learn And Remember Our Presidents   109

Chapter 10 American Facts, People And History   115
Time For A Soundalike   116

Chapter 11 Alphabet Soundalikes And Hooks   123
Difficult To Picture   123
Don't Panic! These Are Easy!   124
Let's Do The First Two Together   124
First Example: A Television Set   125
Important To Review   126
Contract Information As Well   126
No Pressure, But Give It A Shot   130
Still Another Application   130

Chapter 12 Remember Addresses   133
Just Link It All Together   134
Standards Are Important For Addresses Too   134
Multi-Digit Addresses Become A Snap   135
Let's Cut Out A Step   137
Here's An Ideal Example   138
See How You Do   140
Practice For Real-World Application   141

Chapter 13 Remember Telephone Numbers   143
But Let's Make It Even Easier   144
Maybe This One's A Prospect   146
Could Remembering This Number Save A Life?   147

Contents

We Must Get Together   148
Again, Put Yourself To The Test   149
More Real-World Application   150

**Chapter 14 Remember Speeches
                And Sales Presentations   151**
Why Not Just Write It Down?   151
Get A Good Start   152
Back To Basics   152
Link The Key Thoughts...   153
...Or Use The Mental Hooks   154
Now A Bit More Involved   155
Put It In Writing (Or Typing)   156
Seem Familiar?   157
Link The Key Sub-Points   159
Keep Right On Going   160
Don't Sweat It—You're Doing Fine   161
A Great Presentation Still Demands Practice   162
Try The Following   162

Chapter 15 Remember Important Dates   163
It Certainly Couldn't "Hoit"   163
Months Have Their Own Simple Hooks   164
Try A Few Examples   165
Try Some You Might Be Motivated To Remember   166
Days Of The Week Also Have Simple Hooks   167
Anybody Happen To Have The Time?   167
Have Some Fun With These   168
Use Only What You Need   169
You Bet Your Life!   169
You Wouldn't Want To Miss This   170
A Very Worthwhile Skill To Own   171

Chapter 16 Remember What You Read   173
Not A Trick   173
Notice How Easy It Really Is   174
Are You Impressed With Yourself?...You Should Be!   176

Chapter 17 Remember History For School   177

Chapter 18 Remember Those Playing Cards   181
Here's The Demonstration   181
Hooray For Hollywood   182

Contents

Turning The Intangible...Into The Tangible   183
The Others Simply Follow "Suit"   184
Time For A Quick Review   186
Here Are The Cards   186
To Have Mutilated, Or Not To Have Mutilated   188
Try The Rest Yourself   189
Different Forms of Mutilation   189
First Practical Applications For These Techniques   190
You Can Use Your Mental Hooks As Well   190

Chapter 19 Overcome Absentmindedness   191
Let's Explore The Two Kinds   191
Taking The Steps To Improve   192
Has This Ever Happened To You?   192
A String Around Our Brain   193
Where Did I Park That Car?   193

Chapter 20 Apply What You Have Learned   195

*I*NTRODUCTION

May I begin this book with a question? Okay, another question. When you spotted this book, what was your gut reaction? Did you step back and say, "Wow, do I need that!"? If so, then you responded exactly the way I did when I found out that some guy was coming to town to conduct a memory seminar.

I looked at the promotional mailing piece that came to my office and went down the list of memory skills. Looking at all these things, I just knew they were impossible to actually improve upon. There couldn't possibly be a way to significantly improve my ability to retain important facts, phone numbers, addresses and numbers of all kinds. Or become proficient in English and foreign vocabularies and reading comprehension, giving speeches or sales presentations without the use of notes, but especially, **remembering people's names!** There definitely couldn't be a way to almost always remember people's names. Nobody in the world was worse at that than I.

I had tried everything, I thought. I had repeated the names over and over and ov...,well, you get the picture, don't you? I tried writing them down, thinking of others I knew with the same name, and trying to form some association. I finally gave up, after realizing that I was destined to go through life forgetting people's names, embarrassing them and myself, losing business because of it.

On Thursday, Halloween night 1985, I went to a memory seminar in Oklahoma City to listen to Billy Burden of Dallas, Texas.

When I arrived, I spotted my friend, Terry Gunn, and we sat next to each other in one of the front rows. As Terry and I were chatting, Billy Burden entered the room and Terry said, "Yeah, I met him earlier. He seems like a nice guy." As Mr. Burden walked by, he glanced over at Terry and started to say something. Now I was *positive* he was going to say something like "What was your name again?"

Instead, Mr. Burden said, "Hello, Mr. Gunn." And he said it with all the confidence of a man who knew the name of the fellow he was addressing. I freaked out. I realize that doesn't seem like a big deal to you, and it certainly doesn't seem like any big deal to me now. However, back then I was a guy who, nine times out of ten, would literally forget your name while you were telling it to me. Does that ring a bell? But that wasn't the big thing. What he did later in the evening turned out to be the impetus I needed to research this memory-improvement thing until I mastered it. You see, he did what I do now at virtually every one of my seminars and speeches. He asked everyone in the audience whom he had met earlier, for the very first time, to stand up. He then went around the room, calling back everyone's name. He must have called back the names of about a hundred people that night.

I can say this with conviction, not only about myself, but about the many people I have trained. It works. It works. It works! But you must be willing to do two things. Number one, dedicate a reasonable amount of time and effort to learning this system.

Number two, do exactly as I instruct you to do throughout this book. Don't just read it like a novel, but complete the exercises. If you do these two things, you will come away with a memory that is a lot more effective than the one you began with.

So let's turn the page and begin the exciting journey to improving your memory. The first time you go through this book, please do so in sequential order. After that, you can focus on and review the parts where you wish to concentrate. If things get confusing, please stick with it. I will help you master the skills you are about to learn.

Best of success...AND GOOD MEMORIES!

Bob

*C*HAPTER 1

Observation—Association—
(Weird) Imagination

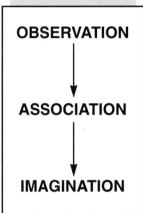

OBSERVATION

↓

ASSOCIATION

↓

IMAGINATION

Memory (dictionary): *The ability to retain and recall past experiences.* **Trained memory (Burg):** *The power to consciously store, retain, and recall past experiences or information, when you want to.*

Memory is a matter of putting together three concepts. Even though the techniques you will learn in order to utilize different memory skills will vary, and at times seem unrelated, they will always involve these three things: OBSERVATION, ASSOCIATION and IMAGINATION.

Begin By Observing

First is observation, or "original awareness." I am a very positive person and I detest the word "impossible." In fact, I pride myself on very rarely using it. However, I am going to use it in a sentence right now. It is impossible to remember, or even forget, anything that we never observed in the first place. That's right! It is impossible to remember or forget anything that we never observed in the first place.

Picture yourself at a party or someplace where you will be meeting new people. In fact, let's make it a business meeting. You see a man walking toward you with a friendly smile and an extended hand. You shake his hand and tell him your name. He says, "Hi, my name is John Malochevski." While you outwardly respond with a smile,

1

you inwardly scream, "AARRRGGGHHHH!!!!!!!! HELP!!!!
I'll never remember this guy's name...
AAAARRRRRGGGGGHHHHH!!!!!!!!"

If you are like most people (as was I) you immediately dropped any
thought of remembering his name. Haven't you done that before?
Not even bothered to observe a person's name because it seemed
difficult? Now, a few minutes, or even seconds later, you must
introduce this new friend or prospect to another person you know
who just happens to be walking over to say hello. Are you
embarrassed because you have already *forgotten* this new person's
name? And because you got so freaked out, you probably don't even
remember that his first name is John. Sound familiar?

So you look down at the name tag. Mr. Malochevski politely smiles
because *everyone does that*. Or if there is no name tag, you
hesitantly ask him to repeat his name, which you probably fail to
observe again. The next time you have to introduce him, you will
really feel average, won't you?

The point is, anytime this has happened in the past, you probably
just shrugged your shoulders and blamed your *poor memory*. But in
reality, your memory was not at fault, because you never actually
observed the name in the first place. And it may not be a difficult
name. You may have been preoccupied at the time. Maybe you were
wondering, "What can I say right now that will make me sound
interesting, wealthy, or intelligent?" We've all done that, haven't
we?

So to improve your memory, you must first use your powers of
observation. Incidentally, observation, as well as the next two
concepts of memory, are learned skills. Observation is a very
important aspect of a well-trained memory, but it is not the only
one.

Next Is Association

If you have ever read a book or a magazine or newspaper article
concerning memory improvement; taken a self-improvement class;
had your mom or dad help you with your homework; attended
elementary, middle or high school; or taken Psych 101 in college,
then you have probably been told that association has a lot to do

with memory. The phrase, "Associate something with something" was probably mentioned more than a few times. On one hand, this is good, because association is an integral part of memory. However, there is one major flaw with this well-intentioned philosophy. The fact is, most people don't realize effective association is much more than "associate something with something." So they attempt to simply associate something with something, and when their ability to recall what they want doesn't dramatically improve, they become discouraged and believe an improved memory isn't possible. I feel it is precisely that lack of understanding regarding the concept of association that has kept the world from knowing just how effective mnemonics (pronounced knee-**mon**-ics, meaning aids to memory) can truly be.

Here's The Answer

The key is knowing how to associate two items, one item you already know with one you wish to remember, in order to make the information stick with you until you wish to recall it. If "associate something with something" were the only key to mastering your memory, then there would be no need for this book. Obviously there is more to it.

One of my favorite stories concerns the time I was at a breakfast function in my hometown of Jupiter, Florida. A man introduced me to a woman by saying, "This is Bob Burg—he *never* forgets a name." Now, first of all, that is not true. Regardless of how effective this system is, it isn't perfect. I can certainly forget a person's name. The woman looked at me, and very *knowingly* said, "Oh, that's association." And she said it in a tone of voice that seemed to say, "I know your secret, you CAD!" I responded with a pleasant smile and said, "It's a pleasure to meet you too." Now, based on her vast knowledge of remembering people's names ("Oh, that's association."), do you suppose she could have gone around the room of about 25 people, most of whom she had just met, and recalled each of their names? Possibly, but I doubt it.

Consider The Following...

Our memory is similar to a computer. In fact, it is quite possibly the most intricate and amazing machine on earth. And like any great computer, its reliability and effectiveness are dependent upon accurate programming and proper input. Do you ever wonder why sometimes you remember things you want to and sometimes you don't? Or why you remember certain things that you would like to forget but can't? And why you sometimes remember an event that took place at age three, but can't remember if you shut the oven off when you left the house an hour ago? Association, in its most basic sense, subconscious association, comes into play here. In fact, it is vital to memory.

But What About Those Everyday Occurrences?

Why don't people remember everyday information as well as they would like to? The answer is very similar to an office filing cabinet. Pretend you have just started a business and bought yourself a beautiful, brand new, clean, empty, never-before-used filing cabinet. Now, on the first day you take the important papers, copies, memos, correspondence, etc. and simply throw them into the filing cabinet in no particular order. The next day you do the exact same thing. In fact, you continue to store your materials in that very same manner. Needless to say, after one week it's cluttered. After two weeks it's messy. After a month it's a disaster area. And a year from now it's a sight that would gross out even a bunch of teenagers.

Now you need to retrieve a document filed soon after you began the business. What happens? You begin digging through what seems like endless miles of clutter, scratching and searching, ripping and reaching. If you happen to get lucky, you eventually find what you wanted. But most likely you give up long before then, realizing that the information is lost to you, maybe not forever, but at least at the moment you need it most. And who is to blame, the filing cabinet?

What If We Changed The Way We Did It?

Now let's alter the story a bit. Still begin with the fact that you just started a business and bought yourself that exact same filing cabinet. Only this time you do something different. You set it up by the day, week, month, year, account number, business name, alphabetically. As you file away your various papers, you do it by the proper category. Again, a full year later, you must attempt to retrieve that very same document. Now what do you do? You go right to the exact location in the cabinet where you *physically* filed it and pull it

out. Simple as that. Does this mean you will never lose a document again? No way! However, you have significantly increased the odds in your favor. It's the same with your memory.

When your memory is trained, you will *mentally* file the information in your *mental* filing cabinet. Does that mean you will never forget anything again? No way! But I promise you will significantly increase the odds in your favor. And that is possible, not through knowing that it is association, but by knowing *how* to associate correctly.

Last, But Not Least, Imagination

Finally, the last concept of memory is imagination, the third part of memory improvement. And after you know how imagination works, it's actually quite fun. You see, once you observe you will associate, and in such a crazy, strange, weird, imaginative way, that you will far more often than not be able to store that information for as long as you want. And then recall it. A portion of the next chapter will be devoted to honing your dormant imagination skills.

A Fun Way To Illustrate

Let's explore a memory technique by playing the game "word association." I say a word (or in this case, write it) and you respond with the very first image or object that comes to your mind. Now to play fair (humor me), you must respond **OUT LOUD**, right away. You might feel a bit silly, but please do it anyway. It's important. Please don't agonize over your response. Just answer as quickly as you can. Besides, any response will be correct, won't it?
All right, here we go:

The first word.....is........... *Thanksgiving*................. What was your reply? Was it turkey, pilgrims, Plymouth Rock or something along those lines? I'm sure it was, but even if it wasn't, it is certain that a picture popped into your mind immediately.

Let's do another one. This time, respond even faster. The next word......is.............*baseball*................... What was your answer this time? Was it a player, a game, the World Series, Reggie Jackson, or something else in that direction? I bet it was. See how easy it is?

Now, let's do just one more. This time though, I want you to respond even faster than the last time. I mean, don't even think about it for a split second. Ready? Here we go..............*July 17, 1980*...
....
.... The long dotted line represents the amount of time that most everyone reading this book took before being able to respond. Now, I know a few of you said "birthday" or "anniversary," and some of you, after thinking real hard for a few quick moments responded with something like "date." But by and large, even though you tried real, real hard to respond as fast as you possibly could, you really couldn't come up with much of anything, could you? Please don't feel bad; you weren't supposed to. *Thanksgiving* and *baseball* are tangible. You can easily see them, picture them in your mind's eye. And because they are pictures with which you are probably familiar, it was easy to respond quickly.

But What's A Date?

On the other hand, *July 17, 1980* are just words, nothing you can get a handle on. And because the event did not represent anything you could see in your mind's eye, you were unable to come back with any kind of quick response.

We Can Picture It

Let's put "July 17, 1980" in a more tangible perspective. Imagine, for instance, that on July 17, 1980, you were somewhere in this country where you could play Lotto. You know, the state lottery game where you pick six numbers and can win lots of money? On the morning of July 17, 1980, you woke up, picked up the newspaper to check the results, and realized you had hit the jackpot. YOU WON 25 MILLION DOLLARS! Unfortunately, you got absentminded (of course, you hadn't yet read chapter 19 of this book) and forgot where you put your ticket for safekeeping. You searched and searched and searched, but realized it was gone forever. And you came to the awful realization that on July 17, 1980, you both won and lost $25,000,000. *Oy Vey!*
Now, back to the present, and I ask you to respond quickly to July 17, 1980. How do you think you would reply? ....
.... Well, honestly, wouldn't "OH SHOOT!" be a

lot more polite? Do you get the point? The intangible words "July 17, 1980" became tangible. And it became something you *knew*.

The key to memory is knowing how to associate two items, one you already know with one you wish to remember. That is this book! Yes, memory is much more than simply "associating something with something."

Observation, Association, And Imagination Are Always Involved In Memory

SUMMARY

When you use these skills, they seem unrelated, but you always use observation, association, and imagination anytime memory is involved. As you go through this book, you will learn a myriad of techniques to better utilize your ability to remember. And even though the techniques for one area of memory improvement might be totally different from another, they will all, yes *all*, be based upon the three concepts of memory—observation, association, and imagination.

Of Chain Links And Soundalikes

The Chain Link Method

Maybe you're acquainted with the Chain Link method of memory. Linking is a basic skill that is taught in almost every memory course. It's as fundamental to a trained memory as throwing a good jab is to boxing. It's just the tip of the memory iceberg, but without the tip, you can't have the rest of the iceberg, can you?

All too often, however, linking is poorly taught. So, when the person who has been exposed to linking attempts to use it in the real world, he or she loses faith in a system that was never given a chance.

The Chain Link method is fun and easy to learn. It is designed for remembering items in sequence. The sequence can be as small as two items or as large as infinity. Chain Linking is based on the fact that memory is the association of two items: one item you already know with another you wish to remember.

Let's Try It

At this time, I am going to give you ten unrelated items. Concentrate on each one, taking up to five seconds before going on to the next. Repeat the process until you finish with all ten objects.

Ready? They are .... thumbtacks .... fish .... car .... restaurant .... Greece.......... magazine.......... mirror .... soccer ball .... quadrangle .... and map. Now, cover them up and decide whether you could go through the list and get most, if not all of them, correct and in sequence. Chances are you couldn't. Perhaps you were able to rattle off the list without a hitch. But could you do it again in an hour? How about 24 hours from now? I'm going to assume you answered no, because from my experience as a memory trainer, I have come to the conclusion that very few people could remember a list of that length without benefit of the Chain Link method.

Let's review this list, making up a story, Chain Linking these items together. This will be accomplished by associating an item you already know with one you want to remember. At that point, the item you want to remember becomes the one you already know. You can then associate that item with another one you wish to remember. Confusing? Linking will make complete sense in just a moment.

Here's How I Would Do It

Our first item was *thumbtacks.* You want to remember thumbtacks, but first you need to associate it with something you already know. Since thumbtacks is the first item, how do we do that? Easy. Associate thumbtacks with yourself. Let's do it this way: In your mind's eye, take off your shoes and see yourself stepping on thousands of gigantic thumbtacks. **Don't just read this, but see it, feel it, experience it.** Can't you feel the pain as all those thumbtacks stick into your feet? So now you *know* thumbtacks. And since thumbtacks has become the item you *know,* you can now associate it with the second object you want to remember, *fish.*

To make this association work, we will again make use of pain as we previously did with thumbtacks. Pain is only one of the six "imagination-association" techniques we will discuss. Now, I love all animals, and consider fish to be animals, and would never want to hurt one. For the sake of this association, however, I am going to ask you to take this gigantic live fish in your mind's eye and slam this fish as hard as you can on those thumbtacks. See them sticking into the fish, and hear the fish screaming in pain.

Now you *know* fish and want to remember *car.* To continue the story, this fish is in so much pain he needs help. So this gigantic (really see it being huge) fish runs, yes, runs, to the car and gets in and drives away.

Now you *know* car and you want to remember *restaurant.* See the fish driving along. After a while, he is no longer in pain, but is very, very hungry. So what does he do? He goes to his favorite restaurant. In your mind's eye, see the fish going to the restaurant and walking in the door. **Critical point: Please don't just read these associations, but see them, feel them, and experience them. Remember that these associations, (especially the ones dealing with pain) are not real, but merely a make-believe movie or cartoon of the mind.**

Now you *know* restaurant, and the next item you want to remember is *Greece,* as in the beautiful country of Greece. In your mind's eye, see this restaurant as having a Greek motif. More than that, go so far as to see this restaurant as being so much like Greece that if you didn't know better, you would think you were really in Greece.

We're Halfway Through

Now you *know* Greece and the next item you want to remember is *magazine.* Let's associate the two this way. This restaurant is so much like Greece that in order not to feel out of place you need a magazine to figure out what is going on. And that's what the waiters supply at each table. Again, "in your mind's eye," (I don't mean to sound like a broken record...broken record...broken record...brok...) see the magazine explaining all about Greece and how to order their food.

Now you *know* magazine and the next item you want to remember is *mirror.* Using your imagination, make believe that this Greek magazine's cover is very shiny, extremely shiny. So shiny, in fact, that if you look into it, you can see your reflection, just like a mirror. See yourself looking at that magazine cover, which becomes a mirror.

Now you know *mirror* and you want to remember *soccer ball.* SMAASSSHHHH! Into a brand-new mirror bounces a soccer ball. And now that soccer ball bounces away. If you saw that picture vividly in your mind's eye then you now *know* soccer ball.

All right, so you *know* soccer ball. What you want to remember next is *quadrangle*, an area surrounded on its four sides by buildings. Guess where this soccer ball is bouncing and rolling? That's right, through a huge quadrangle. And, as it moves, it not only picks up speed, but grows larger and larger.

Now you *know* quadrangle. The last item on the list you want to remember is *map*. Imagine this. The quadrangle turns out to be so incredibly huge that in order to track down the soccer ball you need a map. Unfortunately, as you attempt to unfold your map, it tears into many pieces.

Now you *know* map, and that ends the list. You have completed the entire list using a bunch of silly pictures for which you might not yet see the point. Well, let me ask you to do this. Please cover any information you see on the page before this point. I'm asking you not to look at the list of words or the associations you just went through. Going back to the beginning, to the very first item, try to remember the next item. Don't force yourself to be fast. Just take your time and think about the association. After you have that, go on to the next, and then the next, and continue until you complete your list. If you get stuck, so what? You've only just begun.

And The Results?

How did you do? Did you get every one correct? Or at least most of them? I bet you did. If you didn't, don't worry. But please go back to the first association between *yourself* and *thumbtacks* and really focus on seeing, feeling and experiencing what you are doing. Although the associations *you* make up are going to be a lot more effective than the ones someone else gives you, you should still have gotten a nearly perfect score.

Next, you are going to see what type of imaginative associations are the most effective. But first, I want to impress you with your newly acquired memory skills. Again, cover up all the information that would give you the different items. Starting from the last word, *map,* see how many you can recall by going through the list backwards..................... How did you do this time? Again, I bet you did well. If you feel comfortable with the Chain Link, but still missed one or two items, let me stress right here that the system is not supposed to be perfect. Many times you will get 100% and other times you won't. What the system will do, however, once learned, applied and practiced, is make your memory a heck of a lot more *effective*. A lot more effective than it would be without the system!

Let's Work On Imagination Skills

If you found the exercise extremely easy, great. But I don't expect that's necessarily the case because you have not yet learned the techniques of *making* the association. Let's learn those skills now, using your imagination. Then, if you like, go back and review that last exercise.

You are now going to learn six methods of imagination that help us associate something you already know with something you wish to remember. To reiterate an earlier statement that is so vitally important, once you make an association correctly, the item you wish to remember will then be the one you already know. And at that point you can continue the Chain Link with something new you wish to remember.

Wild And Crazy Pictures

You will notice that the common denominator of every one of these imagination techniques is their illogical nature. Keep in mind that we think in pictures, not words. If I say "banana split," you don't see the letters of those words, but the smooth, creamy ice cream, bananas, delicious toppings, whipped cream, and even a cherry on top, right? Possibly your mouth is watering, just picturing it. Mine certainly is. Advertisers spend big bucks every year giving us pictures to remember. Many of them are crazy pictures. They elicit feelings and emotional responses, which are very memorable. Often, in fact, it's the imagery that we truly hate or find to be hysterically funny, sad, stupid or wacky that stays with us— sometimes years after the ad campaign.

It's...Unforgettable

There is one commercial in particular that comes to mind as I write. It was for a particular sausage, and the invisible voice (a whiny, shrill voice) asking his mother for more of those particular sausages drove me absolutely nutty. I'll tell you what, though: when I think of sausages, that same brand always comes to mind. I'll never forget them, and that is my point. Are there commercials you still remember from when you were younger? Do you remember Alka Seltzer's "I can't believe I ate the_____ _____"? How about "Delta is ready when ____ ____"? And I'll bet there are many more.

Ouch! And More

So, let's begin with the imagination technique of pain. The image of pain is a way to strengthen and eventually remember an association. Do you recall how you felt during the Chain Link exercise when you stepped on all of those thumbtacks with your bare feet? If you truly concentrated as I asked you to and saw that picture in your mind's eye, you probably felt some pain. You then remembered that association when the time came.

The next imagination technique has to do with picturing something really bizarre, something that would never really happen. Do you recall when the item you knew was "fish" and the item you wanted to remember was "car"? In your mind's eye, you saw that fish running to the car and driving away. That's an association that can stay with you easily, isn't it?

Using an exaggerated size, one totally out of proportion, is also an effective technique. Back to our fish running to the car. You may recall he was a gigantic fish. And yes, often we will use not only one, but several techniques for a single association.

The next way we use imagination is substitution. One of the associations was from restaurant to Greece. Restaurant was what you *knew,* and Greece was what you wanted to remember. You may recall that the restaurant had a Greek motif. So much so, in fact, that if you didn't know better, you would have thought you were really in Greece. Substitution also was used when the magazine turned into a mirror.

Still another excellent technique is overstated physical action. For instance, when you wanted to associate mirror with soccer ball, what did you picture? SMAASSSHHHH! Into that mirror bounced a soccer ball. That striking physical action is enough to help you remember that association.

IMAGINATION TECHNIQUES:

Pain

Bizarre

Exaggeration

Substitution

Action

Let's look at the technique of exaggeration of numbers, seeing hundreds or thousands or millions of an item as opposed to the actual amount (which is actually far less). For example, you saw yourself stepping on thousands of thumbtacks. And had you wanted, you could have seen thousands of soccer balls hitting that broken mirror.

Let your imagination soar! It is perfectly all right, and often even more effective, to combine these techniques when forming an association.

Finally—when you can do it—give yourself star billing in your associations. Ham it up. After all, it's your show! When *you* are a player in your own association, the picture has more meaning, thus making it even more memorable.

You Can Quiz Yourself

Now you have seen six examples of imagination techniques that can be used to drive home your associations. I've given you a number of tangible items that you can practice associating. Just remember to use one, or possibly more of these techniques for each association. For continued practice, simply rearrange the words and attempt to associate them in their new order. Or have somebody give you a list to work on. Go slowly at first, and in no time you will be able to associate each item in split seconds. Again, I stress taking the time to do this, not just read it. I assure you, the results will more than make up for the few minutes of extra effort.

The Very Important Soundalike—
For Picturing The Intangible

Now let's look at a concept that I call the *Soundalike.* In the Chain Link exercise, you associated ten items. Each of those items was *tangible,* easily pictured. What you are going to learn now is how to associate two items, even if one or both of them are *intangible,* or difficult to picture. I promise that this will come in most handy when you actually begin using these skills in real life. For right now, however, let's list the names of the presidents of the United States of America, numbers 11 through 20. Try to remember them

Make Yourself the ★

What's a Soundalike?

in sequence. As was the case with the previous list, you have five seconds to study each item, or name, before going on to the next. This list will be tougher than the last; so don't let it bother you, just have fun.

Do you know who the 11th president of the United States was and can you remember it?

Let's begin with the 11th president, whose name was Polk .... the next was Taylor .... then Fillmore .... Pierce .... Buchanan .... Lincoln .... Johnson .... Grant .... Hayes .... and Garfield. Unless already familiar with the names and correct sequence of the presidents, I doubt that anyone, especially me, without knowledge of the techniques, could make all those associations after being exposed to them that one time. Why? Because half of those names didn't present any mental picture.

A Close Look At The Soundalike

What is a Soundalike? A Soundalike is a similar sound or sounds, word or words, that take something you ordinarily cannot picture and turn it into something you *can* picture. A good Soundalike can magically transform the "unpicturable" into an idea that leaps into your lap like a wet spaniel. We know that the names of people like Mr. Malochevski, whom you met earlier, are difficult to remember. Soundalikes serve as tangible reminders of the names. In fact, Soundalikes will come to your rescue in just about every area of memory.

Let's Do It Together

Let's see how it's done. The first president on the list is *Polk.* Since it is first on the list, you need to associate it with something you already know. So hog the show. How do you associate yourself with a vague name like Polk? Try *poke.* Picture yourself having a gigantic index finger and poking yourself in the stomach. You poke yourself so hard with that gigantic finger that it goes right through your body. Ouch! Now, of course, I'm making the associations for you just to help you get started associating intangible items. However, as mentioned earlier, your own associations will always work much better for you.

Now you *know* Polk and you need to associate him with *Taylor.* Picturing a tailor in your mind's eye is fairly simple. It doesn't matter that the name is spelled differently. You can still visualize a tailor, can't you? Picture this kind-hearted tailor using his needle and thread to sew up that hole in your stomach, created when you poked yourself with your gigantic index finger.

Now you *know* Taylor and he needs to be associated with the next president, *Fillmore*. Fillmore is one of those names that, while it cannot actually be pictured, still sounds familiar enough to see when put into sentence form. For instance, you might say to yourself as you see this picture, "A good tailor is able to *fill more* orders for suit repairs than a bad tailor."

Now you *know* Fillmore and you need to associate him with the next president, who was *Pierce*. Pierce could remind us of pierced ears. Just say to yourself as you see this picture, "Fill more of your ears with earrings by repeatedly getting them *pierced*." If it seems kind of silly to you, well ... it is! Just please make sure you are actually doing this along with me, as opposed to simply reading.

Now you *know* Pierce and you need to remember *Buchanan*. Buchanan is certainly a ZAP! Name*, isn't it? But let's handle it with a good Soundalike. How about *two cannons*? We may not be able to picture a "Buchanan," but we can easily picture two cannons, can't we? Now, let's associate Pierce with two cannons. In your mind's eye, see these two cannons being very embarrassed and in pain because someone came along and pierced their ears and put thousands of gigantic earrings on them. Yes, it's bizarre, violent, uses substitution, has the exaggeration of numbers and size, and it will work, if you let it.

Five Down—Five To Go

Moving right along, now that you *know* Buchanan, you need to associate him with the next president, *Lincoln*. The name Lincoln is another one that does not suggest anything we can see or picture.

However, it sounds enough like link, as in a Chain Link, to remind you of the real name. Associating Buchanan, or two cannons, with a

---

*ZAP! Names-Names such as Menelovionis, Abramowicz, Pragaluska, etc., which most of us figure we haven't a chance in the world of remembering anyway, so we just ZAP! right on by them, and don't even try to lock them into our memory.

link on a chain, let's picture thousands and thousands of cannons appearing next to each other, held together by a single, gigantic Chain Link. See those links and you will be reminded of Lincoln.

Now that you *know* Lincoln, you need to associate him with *Johnson*. For Johnson, let's use the Soundalike *yawn sun*, yawn and sun. In your mind's eye, again picture those gigantic Chain Links. One by one, see them begin to yawn from being under the hot sun. The links yawn from the sun. **Just use your imagination.**

Now that you *know* Johnson, you can associate him with the next president, *Grant*. Grant is another one of those names that, even though it cannot necessarily be pictured, still sounds familiar enough to see when put into sentence form. Look up at that hot sun and ask it to grant you the right not to yawn from it. Of course, you don't really have to do that, at least not in public.

Now you *know* Grant. Let's associate him with *Hayes*. The name Hayes does present a mental picture, doesn't it? A *hazy* picture. Just say to yourself as you peer through this haze, "Even though we were granted the right not to yawn from the sun, the weather was still hazy." By the way, you know these sentences don't have to be repeated word for word, just enough to get the picture.

Now that you *know* Hayes, you need to associate him with the final president on the list, *Garfield*. Nowadays, you can just picture Garfield the cat. In your mind's eye, see Garfield wanting to take a nap because it is so hazy outside.

Got The Hang Of It?

Let's go through that list together and see how you do. Please don't panic if you don't get most of them. This was *one tough list* to do the first time using mostly Soundalikes. It was strictly for familiarization to the technique of Soundalikes.

The first president on the list you associated with yourself. If you remember poking yourself in the stomach, you're on the right track. That was Polk.

What was the next association and what was that president's name? Do you recall the kindly tailor sewing up that hole in your stomach? That's right, Taylor.

Who was the next president on the list? If you recalled that a good tailor will fill more orders for suit repairs than a bad tailor, conjure up Fillmore.

And after Fillmore? Could you fill more of your ears by getting them pierced? Enter Pierce. This Chain Link is a lot tougher than the first one, isn't it? Hang in there, though. After cracking these toughies, you will be able to handle anything.

Who was the president after Pierce? What was pierced by thousands of gigantic earrings? If you pictured those two cannons, or even one cannon, then you know it was Buchanan.

And who was the president after Buchanan? What was it that happened to the cannons? Many, many more of them appeared, didn't they? And they were held together by what? If you remembered a link, as in a Chain Link, then you know the next president was Lincoln.

To remember the name of the president after Lincoln, picture what those Chain Links did and why. They must have been awfully tired because they yawned from the sun, and that reminds you of Johnson.

Next, you asked the hot sun a favor. Do you recall what that favor was? The favor was to grant you the right not to yawn from the sun. "Grant" should remind you of President Grant.

Now, even though you were granted the right not to yawn from the sun, what was the weather like outside? Hazy, which reminds you of President Hayes.

Finally, what outlandish fantasy did you spin for the last president on our list? He wanted to take a nap because of the hazy weather. That's right, Garfield the cat. Only in this case, that simply reminds you of President Garfield.

How Did You Do?

If you got most of them right, fantastic. If not, please don't worry. What I would suggest you do, however, is look back to where you associated the first president on the list with yourself. Go through the associations again and really make it a point to see the associations in your mind's eye. I bet you'll do even better this time. And once you know them frontwards, see how many of them you can get in reverse order. Keep in mind that these techniques are not magic. They don't necessarily happen at the snap of a finger. They are a learned skill that becomes easier with practice and experience. Right now, I'm concerned only that you learn and understand the techniques. The ability to use the techniques will come with practice.

Now that you've learned some of the basics and have a foundation to this system, let's play.

CHAPTER 3

TAKE A BREAK!
Test Yourself On Memorabilia

I was very tempted to name this chapter "Create Your Own Luck" because it illustrates that anything at all can be put to memory, if we will just make the effort to do so. In this brief chapter, let's put aside most of the skills we have learned up to this point. Let's look at just a few examples of generic memorabilia.

How would one remember that Mount Fuji is 12,365 feet high? Picture a mountain made of thousands and thousands of gigantic calendars. A calendar represents a year, which, of course, has 12 months, 365 days. That would give you 12,365 feet. Two important things to point out. Again, make sure you *picture* those calendars on the mountain, not just think of them. And if you need to give yourself a stronger hint that it was Mount Fuji, as opposed to just any mountain, then simply put something into your picture to help you out. For instance, you might see that mountain sporting one of those classic oriental-looking mustaches.

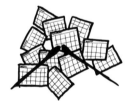

The particular number we want to remember (12,365) is easily associated with something we already know (calendar). It just happens to work out this way, which is lucky for us. However, as mentioned in the first sentence of this chapter, we still had to look for a way to make that luck work for us. For practically any other number, we would need to employ a Mnemonic Alphabet or Mental Hook, which will be discussed later in the book.

MNEMONIC INITIALING

Do you know the names of the five Great Lakes? Even if you think you don't remember them, I'll bet you really do. Picture some lakes in your mind's eye surrounded by gigantic homes. Now take the letters from that word—H-O-M-E-S. The 'H' will trigger off Huron, the "O" Ontario, "M" is for Michigan, "E" will remind us of Erie, and finally "S" for Superior. This is referred to as *mnemonic initialing*, and while at times quite effective, it will only work when you already know the information, and simply need a reminder.

Tell me, is the port side of a boat the left side or the right side? Even if you are like me and know next to nothing about boating, you can remember this answer forever. Simply ask yourself how many letters in the word *port*? And the word, *left*? Each word has the same number of letters. Therefore, we can easily remember that the port side of the boat is the left side. Taking this one step further, is the port side red or green? Well let me ask you this, what color is port wine? Both are red, and there is your answer.

How would one remember that the olfactory nerve has to do with the sense of smell? Picture yourself walking through an old factory, and saying to yourself, "Wow! Does it smell bad!" For this we used our Soundalike technique, didn't we? For the word *olfactory* we used *old factory*.

Let's try incorporating the Soundalike in another example. Several years back, my sister Robyn, who is a professional in the field of Special Education, asked me to help her think of a memory aide that would more easily allow her students to remember the name of the Soviet city Chernobyl, the site of the nuclear catastrophe. I thought about it and came up with this. Picture yourself saying sarcastically, "Gee, it was *sure noble* (Chernobyl) of the Soviet government letting something like that happen." That sentence right there should do it.

What are the four members of a quartet? Let's return to mnemonic initialing, and picture yourself sneaking up behind the quartet with a knife, about to *stab* them. Now let's take those four letters, S-T-A-B, and watch them trigger the answers. The *S* reminds us of Soprano, the *T* of Tenor, the letter *A* helps us come up with Alto, and finally the *B* reminds us of Bass.

Many people know that the sun rises in the east and sets in the west, but many don't. Well, here is an easy way to remember. The word "yeast" can be used as a Soundalike for "east," can't it? Let us then picture filling up the sun with lots and lots and lots of yeast, and watching it rise. Naturally, if we know that the sun rises in the east, then it must set in the west.

A good friend of mine who is politically very active, used to have a difficult time remembering which political party, Republican or Democrat, was represented by which animal, the donkey or the elephant. I told him that remembering that fact was as easy as this. What letter does Democrat begin with? And what letter does donkey begin with? And of course that must mean that Republican is signified by the elephant.

These techniques will come into play even with spelling. I used to have trouble remembering how to spell the last name, Campbell. Did the letter *p* or *b* come first? So I associated that which I wanted to remember how to spell with something I already knew how to spell, and that was the words *camp bell*. I simply said to myself, "When the camp bell rings, all the kids come running for Campbell's soup."

These situations occur almost every day. Remember, if you are willing to create your own system, anything and everything can be put to memory.

CHAPTER 4

Remember People's Names And Faces

"We are all so vain that we love to have our names remembered by those who have met us but once. We exaggerate the talents and virtues of those who can do this and we are ready to repay their powers with lifelong devotion. The ability to associate in the mind names and faces is a tremendous asset to a politician and it will prolong the pastorate of any clergyman."
—*William Lyons Phelps*

Good point Bill ... May I call you Bill?

Actually, I would like to add one thought to Mr. Phelps' splendid observation. Not only will we repay those powers with lifelong devotion, but with our business dollars as well. Really, don't you feel *sooooo* good when someone remembers your name when you don't expect it?

For instance, I know that when I walk into a restaurant with a woman I want to impress (am I really that type?), and the waiter comes over to take our order and says, "Oh, hello Mr. Burg, it's so nice to see you," he is probably going to get a bigger tip than usual. Why? Because he has made me look and feel important, and we all love to look and feel important, don't we? The legendary Dale Carnegie agrees: "Remember that a person's name is to him or her the sweetest and most important sound in any language." And the people who best capitalize on this aspect of human vanity have the greatest chances of winning friends and influencing people—and fattening their bank accounts.

You Can Do It, Too

I get especially excited about the ability to remember people's names because I know that so many people are totally convinced, as I was at one time, that mastering this skill, or even improving it, is next to impossible. Well, it isn't. In fact, it's not only possible, but fun as well.

Gee, I Remember Your Face, But...

Let us first take a quick moment to answer one of the most often asked questions I come across. Actually, it is more of a statement than a question. It goes something like this: "Bob, I'm great at remembering faces. I'll tell you what, I can meet someone, and it doesn't matter how long until I see that person again, I will still remember his/her face, but for the life of me, I cannot remember his/her name." I guess the question is, Why is it I can remember faces but not names? Good question! Here's a good answer. The reason faces are memorable is that faces are tangible. You certainly wouldn't look at a person and say, "Y'know, I remember your name, but I just can't quite remember your face," would you? Of course not. And why? Because again, faces are tangible, faces have handles. Names, on the other hand, are intangible; they cannot be seen. They are merely sounds, air, nothing, zero, nada, goornisht.

When we walk up to a person we have met previously, we still see the same face, but unless that person is wearing a name tag we do not see the name. What we need to learn how to do is to not only be able to see that person's name (and I'm not talking about name tags), but to be able to connect it with that person's face as well. In order to make name/face connections effectively, we must follow these six steps (please glance at them quickly, and then continue):

Six Steps to Remembering Names

1. Observe the person's outstanding facial feature.

2. Exaggerate the person's outstanding facial feature.

3. Observe the person's name.

4. Repeat the person's name (in order to ensure you heard it correctly).

5. Form a mental picture of what the name suggests, or a Soundalike (a similar sound or sounds, word or words, which take something you cannot picture, and turn it into something you can picture).

6. Form a ridiculous association between the mental picture suggested by the name or Soundalike and the outstanding facial feature (use your great imagination, and even a phrase, if necessary).

Attack Them One-By-One

All right, so let's take each of these steps individually, and see how they all lead to mastery of remembering names and faces.

The Face Is Very Important

First, we need to observe the person's outstanding facial feature. When I use the term "outstanding facial feature," I do not necessarily mean the outstanding good feature or outstanding bad feature, but simply the feature on that person's face that stands out the most, or is most prominent. An outstanding facial feature could be almost anything: big eyes, small eyes, deep-set eyes, almond shaped eyes, big nose, small nose, pug nose, thin eyebrows, thick eyebrows, wrinkly forehead, high forehead, thin face, long face, round face, small scar, big scar, thin lips, thick lips, character lines from the nose, dimple, mustache, beard, bald head, curly hair, square chin, high cheekbones, low cheekbones, freckles, and the list goes on and on. In fact, it is actually limitless, depending upon how diligently you look.

Just a friendly warning, however: often, as we are beginning the process of noticing and picking out outstanding facial features, we look at the person we are about to meet and say to ourselves, "Hey, what am I going to do? This person doesn't have an outstanding facial feature. His/her face is totally plain." Well, just so you won't panic when that time comes, don't worry. That person does in fact have an outstanding facial feature; it is simply a matter of getting used to how to find it, which gets easier and easier.

Step number two is to exaggerate the person's outstanding facial feature. Now that we have isolated it, we are going to use our imagination and make it really stand out. In other words, if the person has big eyes, see those eyes as being huge. If the person's eyes are small, then in your mind's eye see them as being tiny. If he has a thin face, see that face as being so thin that a toothpick would have trouble hiding behind it. If she has a scar, then see that scar as being extremely deep. Whatever the person's outstanding facial feature, simply see it as being much more than it really is.

Make Sure To Get The Name

Step number three is to observe the person's name. I know, that sounds like such a simple step, but how many times do we overlook doing that for one reason or another? We covered several of those reasons in Chapter 1, including the fact that up until this point in our lives, we were so used to not remembering names, conveniently blaming our *poor memory*, that we expected to fail, and thus did not even bother to observe the name in the first place. Then there is the seeming difficulty of being able to picture that person's name, a skill we will master very soon. Until now, though, we have dealt with the person's name by simply deciding *not* to deal with it, or even to observe it at all. So from now on, please observe the person's name when you hear it.

Step number four is to repeat the name. The main reason for repeating is to ensure you heard it correctly in the first place. For example, if you hear a couple tell you their name is Smith, and you say, "Hello Mr. and Mrs. Smith," then, fine. However, if their name is really pronounced Schmidt, and you just heard it as Smith, then they will correct you right there. And both they and you will feel good about the fact that you now have their name correct. If, when they tell you their name, you don't hear it clearly enough to be sure you know it, then simply ask them to repeat it. Some people tell me they feel embarrassed to do that, but believe me, if there is one thing I know, it is the fact that not only will they not feel offended by your asking, but they will take it as a tremendous compliment that you cared enough to make sure you heard their name correctly. You can also repeat the name once or twice during the conversation just to get familiar and comfortable with it. "Nice to meet you, Mr. and Mrs. Schmidt." Or maybe, "You certainly have a beautiful daughter, Mrs. Schmidt; in fact, I believe she looks just like her mother."

Now, don't chant their name. It won't look good to stare at them and repeat, "Schmidt, Schmidt, Schmidt, Schmidt, Schmidt," (I say that tongue-in-cheek, of course) and besides, that sort of rote memorization isn't going to work anyway. Better to simply repeat the name once when you hear it, then maybe once or twice during the conversation, and once again when ending the conversation.

Handling The Name Part

Step number five is to form a mental picture of what the name suggests, or a Soundalike— a similar sound or sounds, word or words, which take something you cannot picture and turn it into something you can picture. The Soundalike will simply serve as a reminder of the real name. Now, there are many names that do present pictures. Please glance at the names in the upper left column of the next page. Each of these names suggests pictures that we can easily see. On the other hand, there are many, many names that by themselves do not present pictures. A short list of these appears in the right column of the next page. A longer list of Zap! Names (1000 of them, to be exact) appears at the end of this chapter. They are yours to familiarize yourself with, and to make mastering this name-remembering system much faster and easier. You will find that you do not have to rely on "hard core" memory. As long as you are familiar and comfortable with how the Zap! Names become items you can picture, the purpose will be served. I have also included 100 first names, as well as various "standards" for different parts of names. The same will hold true with these as with the last names.

ZAP!

Names that suggest pictures	Names for which we need Soundalikes
Taylor	Gordon—garden
Horne	Kakish—cactus
Carr	Sullivan—sell a van
Frost	Foster—force tear
Sanders	Colletti—call a tea
Walker	Garrett—carrot
Coleman	Marcott—my cot
Miller	Nixon—nicks on, mixin'
Hunter	Henderson—hand her some
Forrest	Quigley—wiggly
Rose	Martin—my tin
Hill	Harackiewicz—hairy carrots
Pierce	James—games
Colby	Thibodeau—tip a doe
Wolf	Van vliet—van fleet
Silverman	Zarkin—far in, parkin'
Carpenter	Connolly—corn'l leave
	Bennett—pen net
	Frazier—razor
	Simon—dime in
	Rondeau—run doe
	Berrisano—berry sand o
	Murphy—more peas
	Kaplan—cap land
	Leonhardt—lean hard
	Jones—stones
	Giargregorio—gin in cracked car
	Malinowski—mail on a ski
	Sannicandro—sunny can grow

Now Lock It In

The sixth and final step is what really ties it all together. Form a ridiculous association between the mental picture suggested by the name, or Soundalike, and the outstanding facial feature. Use your great powers of imagination, and even a phrase, if necessary.

Let's Walk Through Two Examples

For practice, let's meet some people right now. We don't even need to actually look at their faces at this time; you will picture them easily. I'll walk you through the first two, then ask you to try some on your own.

Let's pretend that you are about to be introduced to a woman who has somewhat deep-set eyes. Before you are even introduced to her, you observe that her outstanding facial feature happens to be those deep-set eyes. Now exaggerate the outstanding facial feature, and see this woman's eyes being extremely deep-set. Wow, her eyes are so deep-set, they are way back in their sockets. Now, as the two of you shake hands, you observe her telling you that her name is Joan Forrest. For right now don't concern yourself with her first name; we will work on that later. Now, repeat her name so it fits naturally into the conversation, such as, "It's very nice to meet you, Ms. Forrest." The next step is to form a mental picture of what the name suggests, or, if the name doesn't suggest anything you can easily picture, decide upon a Soundalike that would work. In this case, the name "Forrest" is easy to picture, isn't it? Simply picture a forest. The fact that the two words are not spelled exactly alike does not even come into play. Picturing a forest will work just fine.

The final step is to form a ridiculous association between the forest and her deep-set eyes. I would see those deep-set eyes of Ms. Forrest actually being a huge forest with thousands and thousands of gigantic trees in them. I would also try to put myself into that picture by walking around in there, and possibly getting lost.

Maybe I would even say to myself, "It sure would be easy to get lost in that huge forest inside Ms. Forrest's deep-set eyes." A pretty easy one, isn't it? However, be especially careful with the easy pictures. Surprisingly, the easy pictures are the ones we forget, as we tend not to concentrate as hard with them.

Let's try another one. This time, the person you are about to meet is a man whose outstanding facial feature happens to be character lines coming from each side of his nose. In reality, they are not especially deep; however, since they are his outstanding facial feature, you see them in your mind's eye as being extremely deep. You observe as he tells you that his name is Dave Frazier. You respond by repeating his name, and then you immediately decide if Frazier is a name you can picture, or if a Soundalike is needed. In this case, a Soundalike appears to be needed, doesn't it? It would be awfully difficult to picture a frazier. Now you might be thinking, well, what about Joe Frazier, the former heavyweight boxing champion, or even my good friend who also happens to be named Frazier?

Let me say right here that although there are different theories regarding the use of celebrities or others we may know with the same name as the person we are trying to remember, I personally discourage it. Why? Because it gets confusing. If someone you meet for the first time is named Steven Sinatra, and you picture Frank, that might be fine while he is still right in front of you. But chances are that when you see that person again the next day or week, you won't be sure whether he told you his name was Mr. Sinatra or Mr. Martin (as in Dean). You might remember that you pictured a celebrity, but which one?

Anyway, back to Mr. Frazier. A good Soundalike for Frazier is *razor*. It sounds enough like the real name to serve as a reminder, yet is much easier to picture. Now you must make a weird association between the character lines and the razor. If it were I making the association, I might see Mr. Frazier at one time having no character lines, but after I shaved that area enough times with my gigantic razor, his character lines began to form. And of course the more I did it, the deeper those character lines became. Or you might see yourself trying as hard as you can to shave off his character lines with your gigantic razor. Whichever association you use, really see the picture clearly in your mind's eye. Even see the details of the particular razor: the color, brand, size, etc. And you are probably waiting for me to say that the association *you* make will, of course, work best for you.

Continuing On, Without Even Any Pictures

Now I will give you the outstanding facial features and then the names of eight people. Make sure to go through all six steps with each person (yes, even repeating the name out loud). After these next eight people, we will review all ten to see how you did. I will give you the associations I would have made for these eight, but if you think you have one that would work better, then please use it. If these seem difficult at all, please don't worry! You are again learning something new. I am not concerned with the number you get right, only that you begin to feel more comfortable with the procedure.

Let's Review the Six Steps to Remembering Names

1. Observe the person's outstanding facial feature.

2. Exaggerate the person's outstanding facial feature.

3. Observe the person's name.

4. Repeat the person's name (in order to ensure you heard it correctly).

5. Form a mental picture of what the name suggests, or a Soundalike (a similar sound or sounds, word or words, which take something you cannot picture, and turn it into something you can picture).

6. Form a ridiculous association between the mental picture suggested by the name or Soundalike and the outstanding facial feature (use your great imagination, and even a phrase, if necessary).

The first person you are about to meet is a woman with hairy eyebrows. Her name is Hazel Gold. All right, let's make the association.

See her hairy eyebrows filled with thousands of gigantic nuggets of gold. Can't you see yourself just taking all those nuggets of gold right out of Ms. Gold's hairy eyebrows? You should be real wealthy after doing that.

You are about to meet a gentleman with a very round face. His name is Tim Simon. A good Soundalike for Simon is *dime in*. See Mr. Simon's face being so round because it was stuffed (possibly by you, to make the association even more meaningful) with lots and lots of gigantic dimes.

Now imagine his round face getting skinnier and skinnier as the dimes begin shooting out of his face.

The next person is a woman with dimples on either side of her face. Her name is Mary Garrett. For Garrett, you might want to picture a *carrot*. Garrett and carrot sound alike, don't they?

In your mind's eye, you can picture a gigantic carrot sticking out of each of her dimples. The already huge carrots continue to grow larger and larger. Really force yourself to see this picture. It gets easier with practice.

Now you are about to meet a man with a very scraggly mustache. This brings up the question, "Bob, how can facial hair count when it might not be there the next time you see him?" I will answer that question with another question. Have you ever known a person who had a mustache or beard, shaved it off, and it was about a week later before you realized that the man had shaved? Amazing but true, isn't it? Because of that phenomenon, facial hair does count as an outstanding facial feature. And if you should ever find that it doesn't work for you, then by all means don't use it. However, I would encourage you to use it for right now. It will usually work.

This man's outstanding facial feature is his scraggly mustache. His name is Mark Taylor.

> Simply picture it taking a very skillful tailor to mend Mr. Taylor's scraggly mustache. Make sure you can see the picture, and make it as silly and illogical as you possibly can.

Our next person is a woman whose outstanding facial feature is her high cheekbones. Her name is Eileen Rose. I would suggest seeing yourself attempting to plant hundreds of roses in her high cheekbones.

> After finally getting them all planted, they one by one begin to fall out, but you do your best to replant them. Silly? Of course. The sillier the better.

Let's introduce ourselves to a gentleman who has an extremely pointed nose. His name is Norman Kakish. We need a Soundalike for Kakish, don't we? Picturing *cactus* will do just fine. Let's use substitution to remember his name.

> Imagine that pointed nose actually being a *cactus*. If you touch it (only in your mind's eye of course, in order to avoid the possibility of Mr. Kakish touching your nose...with his fist) you will probably stick your finger on one of the needles. The Soundalike *cactus* will probably remind you of his real name, which is Kakish.

Your business associate is about to introduce you to a gentleman whose outstanding facial feature is obviously his receding hairline. His name is Paul Walker.

> Make that association by seeing yourself walking on the top of his forehead for so long that he lost all of the hair he had in that area, and now he has a receding hairline. Really see it happening.

And finally, you are about to meet a woman with very tiny ears. She tells you her name is Terri Malinowski. A Soundalike for Malinowski might be *mail* (a postal letter) *on a ski*.

> Try to imagine the difficulty a piece of mail would have skiing down Ms. Malinowski's tiny ears. Try and make that ridiculous picture really come alive. You might have used *melon ow ski* for your Soundalike, and pictured a melon yelling "OW!" as it attempted to ski down Ms. Malinowski's tiny ears.

I Bet You Remember Them

All right, we have met a total of ten people, without the benefit of even seeing their faces. Here is what I would like you to do. Go back to the first introduction and very briefly review each of the associations, just concentrating on remembering the last names. But don't put too much pressure on yourself.

After your review, please attempt to fill in the blank next to the outstanding facial features listed below which are out of sequence. As you come to each outstanding facial feature, simply picture your association, and then your true memory should supply you with the correct name.

(woman) Dimples_____	(man) Receding hairline_____
(man) Thin nose _____	(man) Round face _____
(man) Character lines _____	(woman) Tiny ears _____
(woman) Deep-set eyes _____	(woman) High cheekbones _____
(woman) Thick eyebrows_____	(man) Scraggly mustache _____

How did you do? Did you get them all correct? Most of them? A few of them? None of them? Again—it doesn't matter. I just want you to get the hang of it. At the conclusion of the chapter, I will supply you with some good practice exercises that will help you to steadily improve your real-life "names and faces" abilities.

Just Like Learning How To Drive A Car

At this point, I am reminded of learning to drive a "standard shift" car. If you can drive a standard shift car, you will probably be able to relate to this analogy. Do you recall the very first time you attempted to drive a standard shift car? Crunch, lurch, stall. Wasn't that first hour something awful? If you were anything like me, you were so concerned with trying to coordinate the releasing of the clutch with the handling of the gearshift, you weren't actually going anywhere. After that first hour, however, it was a bit easier, wasn't it? And it became progressively easier with each trip behind the wheel. Eventually, you were able to drive that car by instinct, the individual steps blending together as one fluid motion. This method of remembering names and faces works the same way.

First Names Are Even Easier

Now to learn how to remember people's first names. There are actually two ways, depending upon the circumstances. First, if you need to remember only the first name of the person you are meeting, simply use the same method you just learned for remembering the last name. It will now be much easier to do.

Now, however, let's return to the business world, or any other situation where it would be prudent and certainly more impressive to remember both the first name and last name. I have found, by the way, that most everyone (even if they won't admit it) appreciates being referred to by their last name, preceded, of course, with Mr. or Ms. Depending upon the situation, I personally address people by Mr. or Ms. until they ask me to call them by their first names. And I have been complimented for that practice. Besides, if I am going to err, I would rather do it on the side of respect and courtesy.

So, assuming that we desire to remember both first and last names, here is how it is done. Lock in the person's last name exactly as you learned. At that point, the last name becomes what you already know. What you want to remember is the first name. We learned about that relationship in Chapter 1. Take the picture you now have of the person's last name and associate that with the picture of the first name. Let's do that for the ten people we just met.

Joan Forrest—For Joan, I use *groan.* Your original picture is of being lost in that forest. I don't know about you, but being lost in a forest would certainly make me groan—real loud.

Dave Frazier—For Dave, I use *save.* Go back to the picture of shaving off those character lines with a razor (Frazier). You keep doing that, as Mr. Frazier hopes someone will come along and save him from any more.

Hazel Gold—For Hazel, I simply picture a *hazelnut.* We saw ourselves picking gigantic gold nuggets out of Ms. Gold's hairy eyebrows. Imagine that one of those nuggets turns out to be a hazelnut. How disappointing, right? Again, that is almost so logical that you might forget. Somehow make yourself see that hazelnut in a weird and illogical way.

Tim Simon—For Tim, *tin* will work fine. We had seen the gigantic dime in (Simon) Mr. Simon's very round face. In fact, there were lots of them, weren't there? Well, the strange thing about these dimes is that they were all wrapped in tin foil.

Mary Garrett—For Mary, I use *marry.* For this, you can picture a ring or a wedding veil. We know that gigantic carrots (Garrett) sticking out of Ms. Garrett's dimples reminded us of her true last name. In this instance, I might say to myself, "I sure wouldn't want to marry a woman who has gigantic carrots sticking out of each of her dimples." (I mean really, it's one thing for her to have small or medium size carrots sticking out of her dimples, but not gigantic ones.)

Mark Taylor—For Mark, I use either a *Magic Marker*™ or simply the picture of a physical mark. In this instance, where it took a skillful tailor to mend Mr. Taylor's scraggly mustache, I might just see him taking his *Magic Marker*™ and marking up the spots that needed the most repair.

Eileen Rose—For Eileen, I just see myself leaning (I lean). You might say to yourself, as you see this picture, "If I lean on all of those roses, surely they will be crushed beyond repair."

Norman Kakish—For Norman, I use *normal* and associate that with the last name. For instance, in this particular case I might ask myself, "If a nose like Mr. Kakish's was actually made out of cactus, would that be normal?"

Paul Walker—For Paul, I use *ball*. You saw yourself walking on the top of Mr. Walker's forehead for so long that he lost all of the hair he had in that area, and now he has a receding hairline, correct? Now you could also picture that while you were walking, you were bouncing a gigantic basketball. I'm sure that didn't help his hair any.

Terri Malinowski—For Terri, I picture a *terry cloth*. Remember that letter (mail) on a ski? Or even the melon saying "OW!" as it attempted to ski down those tiny ears? Whichever association you used, just put a terry cloth into the picture. And be sure to make it illogical.

Now let's quiz ourselves on the first names. I will give you the last names and you fill in the blanks.

Garrett _____	Kakish _____
Forrest _____	Simon _____
Malinowski _____	Frazier _____
Walker _____	Rose _____
Taylor _____	Gold _____

If you made it a point to really concentrate on either the associations I gave you or your own, and allowed your imagination to run a bit wild, then I'm sure you scored high. If you're not quite satisfied with the results, then review the associations one more time and test yourself again; I know you will do even better.

Let's Meet Some Real Folks

If you did well in associating these people's last names with their outstanding facial feature, then this next part will be even easier. Let's face it, you still had to imagine a face, and that isn't always easy. Now, let's meet some people whose faces we can at least see, even if they are only two-dimensional pictures. Real faces are actually much easier, once you get comfortable with this method.

With each picture, you will have the first and last names, and suggested Soundalikes for last names (standards for first names are in the back of this chapter), as well as that person's occupation. Go through the six steps in order to remember each person's last name. Please make it a point to cover up the person's name until you observe and then exaggerate the outstanding facial feature. When you feel you know the person's last name, then lock in the first name. Finally, try to come up with a way to lock in that person's profession. After you do each of these yourself, please look at the way I made the associations. *Remember,* if I seem to have the hang of it more than you do right now, it is only because I have been doing it longer. You will catch on. Besides, the following names are not exactly the easiest you will ever come across. I am attempting to make this as realistic for you as possible. (Especially considering the fact that *most* people we meet in life are actually alive, breathing, and three dimensional...at least physically.)

Bill McCue (construction worker)—The outstanding facial feature I used for Mr. McCue was his wide nose. I took *my cue* stick (McCue) and shoved it as hard as I could up his wide nose. Wow, that must have hurt! I'm sure he wanted to take a *pill* (Bill) in order to relieve the pain. I was able to put his profession, construction worker, into the picture by imagining that this incident took place out on the construction site where a billiards table was set up.

That's where I shoved my cue stick up his nose. What a strange guy I am to be able to come up with that scenario, right? Well, maybe. But more than that, I am simply using the techniques you have been learning from the beginning of this book. If your associations didn't work, then just go over them again, this time even stronger. Or, you can even use mine.

Gwendolyn Smith (hospital administrator)—I used the mark on the left side of her face as her outstanding facial feature. Knowing that my standard for Smith is a *blacksmith's* hammer, I simply saw the mark on Ms. Smith's face being chiseled out by that blacksmith's hammer. For Gwendolyn, I use *dwindlin'*. See that mark as having once been very large, but now, fortunately for Gwendolyn, it is dwindlin' down in size. Dwindlin' should remind you of Gwendolyn, especially after you have used that for several different women named Gwendolyn. To work her profession, hospital administrator, into the picture, I see her running down the halls of the hospital with her blacksmith's hammer, threatening to wreak havoc upon anyone not working. Now please keep in mind that Ms. Smith might be the nicest, sweetest, kindest hospital administrator in the entire world, and that we are making our association only to serve our immediate purpose, and that is to remember her name.

Don Carson (professional baseball player)—I immediately see the beard as being Mr. Carson's outstanding facial feature. The name Carson, if you divide it into syllables, presents the picture of a *car* and the *sun*. No Soundalike is needed. You might even see a car and a smaller car (its son). Whatever you feel comfortable with. In this case, I am going to use car and sun. Let's put one of those old Matchbox Cars in that beard, and see it being totally protected from the sun. You might even say to yourself, "Inside Mr. Carson's beard, a car would definitely be protected from the sun." My standard for the first name Don is *pawn,* as you might find in a chess set. See that car, which is protected from the sun, being driven by a gigantic chess pawn. Mr. Carson is a professional baseball player, and to work that into the picture, simply see that gigantic pawn driving his car to the stadium, in order to get ready for the big game.

Tanya Reagan (physical therapist)—You may have noticed the low cheekbones on Ms. Reagan, as I did. Of course, you also may not have, because as you know, ten or more of us could look at the same face and each see a different outstanding feature. But I used her low cheekbones, and for Reagan I used *ray gun*. See Ms. Reagan's cheekbones being so low because you shot them with a ray gun. That would definitely make them sag real low, wouldn't it? To work in her first name, which is Tanya, you might pretend that the effect of the ray gun turned her cheekbones *tan* in color. Say to yourself, this'll really tan ya, Tanya Reagan. Ms. Reagan is a physical therapist. Easy, right? After having her cheekbones lowered by that ray gun, she would definitely need physical therapy.

James Conant (reporter)—The outstanding facial feature I see for Mr. Conant is his triangular-shaped face. Hmm, ... doesn't that triangular-shaped face sort of suggest an ice cream *cone*? In fact, what if you took a gigantic ice cream cone, topped with *ants* instead of sprinkles? If you can use your imagination and picture that, then simply substitute that ice cream *cone* with *ants* instead of sprinkles for the shape of his face, and you have your association. Jim is a nickname for James, for which the standard I use is *games*. If you can remember James, your natural memory will trigger off whether he likes to be referred to as James or Jim. See those ants on top of that cone playing lots of games in the ice cream, and you have his first name remembered. He is a reporter. To remember that, picture Jim thinking that somebody ought to report what is going on in that ice cream.

Joanne Di Atillio (dietitian)—I see Joanne's outstanding facial feature being her short, curly hair. As you know, for Di Atillio, I picture a gigantic golf *tee* (Di), *tilling*, or hoeing a bunch of Cheerios™. Really use your imagination for this one. Now, you know that for the first name, Joanne, I use *chowin'*. In your mind's eye, picture Joanne chowin' on those Cheerios™. And it just happens that Joanne is a dietitian, which fits perfectly into this picture, doesn't it?

Were You Wondering...?

Please allow me a second to answer a question that you may have thought about. "Bob, some of these associations really fit in with each other, and some of the last names even fit in with the outstanding facial feature. Did you do that on purpose to make it easier for us?" The answer is definitely "no." For the most part, they are fitting because you are making them fit. Some do fit in more logically than others, but hey, if they do, give yourself a break and jump on the obvious, as long as it follows the six steps. By the way, if you are finding these easy, congratulations, because—they *ain't*.

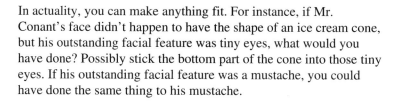

In actuality, you can make anything fit. For instance, if Mr. Conant's face didn't happen to have the shape of an ice cream cone, but his outstanding facial feature was tiny eyes, what would you have done? Possibly stick the bottom part of the cone into those tiny eyes. If his outstanding facial feature was a mustache, you could have done the same thing to his mustache.

What I am saying is this. These six steps will work as long as you allow yourself to *make* them work. As far as the easy or natural associations go, if you get one, take advantage of it. Just be sure to make the association as illogical as you can in order to make it more memorable. Enough said.

Ed Marconi (teacher)—The shape of Mr. Marconi's face was what I saw as his outstanding facial feature. To me, his face sort of angles down into a square chin. The Soundalike for Marconi being *macaroni,* simply see yourself pulling a gigantic piece of macaroni out of his face through that square chin. You might also say to yourself as you see the picture, "I am going to pull this piece of macaroni out of Mr. Marconi's face through his square chin." His first name is Ed, for which I use *egg.* Just see that particular piece of macaroni being egg macaroni. To work into the picture the fact that Ed Marconi is a teacher, I suggest you picture him teaching us how to make egg macaroni from scratch.

Dianne Collibus (salesperson)—For Ms. Collibus' outstanding facial feature I see her small mouth. You need to find a bus to get to work, and you know there is one inside Ms. Collibus' mouth. Just *call a bus,* and one will probably drive right out of Ms. Collibus' small mouth. Strange picture, and it will work!

For Dianne, the standard I use is *die ant.* Which is exactly what would happen to an ant that was standing in front of that bus. Let's hope that doesn't happen. Ms. Collibus happens to be a salesperson. If that ant is a good enough salesperson, perhaps it can talk its way out of being run over by that bus.

Take These Techniques To Heart

There we have it. Review your examples as often as you need to feel comfortable with them. Meanwhile, I would like to give you some good practice techniques for becoming proficient in this challenging and crucial area of memory. Use the following practice techniques and the method you have learned will work like a charm.

First The Face...

For the next seven days, I am going to ask you to note and exaggerate the outstanding facial feature for everyone with whom you come into contact. Don't worry yet about remembering their names, just observe and exaggerate their outstanding facial features. Do this whether they are people you are seeing for the first time or have known most of your life; whether they are business associates or members of a group, club or organization to which you belong. And, of course, this also goes for pictures in newspapers and magazines. Get yourself used to picking out the outstanding facial feature in everyone. At first, it may seem difficult to find an outstanding facial feature on everyone. And sometimes it may take a while. So what? They will never know what you are doing. Besides, you aren't yet trying to remember their names, so for right now, take as long as you need to isolate and exaggerate that feature. You will pick up speed very quickly. Remember the standard shift. It won't take long.

Then The Name

Also during this first week, at your convenience, look over the 1000 Soundalikes at the end of this chapter and familiarize yourself with them. After seeing the mental pictures for these Soundalikes several times, you will feel much more comfortable with them. At that point, begin glancing through your telephone book to check out the different names and attempt to make up Soundalikes for those that do not present pictures. After you feel more comfortable, begin trying to come up with mental pictures and Soundalikes for those people you meet, while you are meeting them, including people you know and pictures of people in newspapers and magazines.

At that point, which is maybe a week or two from now (don't rush it; go at a comfortable pace), you will be going through five of the six steps you have learned in this chapter. If from now on you only followed those first five steps, you would still greatly increase your ability to remember names and faces, because of the concentration you have put forth just to get that far. But we want to go the whole nine yards, and really make it work.

Practice
Practice
Practice
Practice
Practice
Practice

Slowly Bring Them Together

My suggestion: For one week, make a conscious effort to meet and remember the name and face of *one new person* every day. One new person. While you are doing that, you can also do another exercise that will greatly help you to get used to that "standard shift" problem we all have while learning the skill. Look through your newspaper, or a magazine, and take a pair of scissors and literally cut out 10-20 pictures of people whose names you do not know. Without looking at the names, fold them under the picture. If the name doesn't happen to be under the person's picture, but somewhere else on the page, then write the name on the back of the picture. Then one by one, slowly at first, go through the six steps to remembering each person's name. After every few, review them quickly and then go on, until you have done them all. You know it will get easier and faster as time goes on.

Back to real live people. Once you have mastered remembering one new person's name per day, go on to two, then three, then four, and so on and so on. Don't expect to bat 1000. The last professional baseball player to even bat over .400 was Ted Williams, who batted .406 in 1946.

Enhance Your Networking

All right, so we are a bit further down the road. Again, whether it is a week, two weeks, a month, or two months, it doesn't matter. You can walk into that party or the Chamber of Commerce meeting and blow people away by meeting them and then remembering and calling them by their names. Wow! Can't you picture it happening? Well, it will. Just follow these instructions.

When you arrive, walk over to a person and introduce yourself. Lock in that person's name. Then go on to the next person and do the same thing. Now do that with another person and you have met three people, and you remember them. At this point, make sure you remember them by glancing back and reviewing them. Yes. Nothing wrong with that; they will not know what you are doing.

Proceed to the next two or three people, then look back and review everyone you have met up to this point. Probably five or six, right? Now continue meeting people one at a time, pausing after every few to run a quick review of those you've met. Use your own judgment. You won't have to review every person every time, but when you get a chance, do it. One friendly warning I might give you is not to memorize too large a group your first time. Begin with 10-15. Next time 15-20, and after that, dare to be spectacular. Actually, however many people you happen to feel comfortable trying to memorize is just fine. After repeating this exercise many times, you will master the skills.

Now, make sure you discreetly show off your newly acquired ability. Example: one of the first people you met was Charlene Foster. Forty-five minutes later you walk past her at the hors d'oeuvres table. You glance at her and say, "Hi, Ms. Foster, are you enjoying yourself?" She (having no idea of what your name could possibly be) will most likely be quite impressed. Do this with a few more people, and word about you, the one who remembers *everybody's name*, will get around.

Two Final Quick Points

I would like to answer a couple of questions you may have. The first question is, "Bob, what if I am introduced to several people at the same time?" Gosh, you ask some good questions. The answer is try to avoid that type of situation as often as possible. If there are two people, you can just try to concentrate that much harder, but it can be tough. Any more than two or three people at one introduction, and I simply make a point of concentrating on their outstanding facial features. As the group begins to disperse, I approach each of the people individually and inform them that, "The names were said much too quickly for me to observe them all, but I like to make it a point to remember people's names. May I please ask for yours again?" Let me tell you something. Just doing that earns you a point in that person's book for professionalism and likability. And those qualities spell social and professional SUCCESS!

> *"The pessimist sees the difficulty in every opportunity. The optimist sees the opportunity in every difficulty."*
> *L. P. Jack*

After that individual person tells you his/her name, you lock it right in, and then *remember* it. That ensures your success. Incidentally, if your goal at a function you are attending is to meet and remember as many people as possible, try to be the first person there. That way, you will get to meet a core group of early arrivers, which will give you an extra edge.

The second question is, "How long will I keep in my mind these weird images of the people I am meeting?" As with all the other associations we make in order to remember facts, dates, numbers, etc., you will see these weird images or pictures only for as long as you need them. After the second or third time you meet a new person, his or her name will become "true memory," and the weird associations will no longer be needed.

Go out and do it! I'm proud of you already.

Quick Reference — First Name Soundalikes

Men's First Names

Andrew—Ant rules (ruler)
Anthony—A toe knee
Bernie—Burn knee
Bill—Pill, dollar bill
Brad—Brat
Bruce—Juice
Carl—Cow
Charles—Jowels
Chris—Crisco™, crisp
Clete—Baseball cleats
Darren—Tearin'
Daryl—Towel
Dave—Save
Dennis—Menace
Don—Pawn
Doug—Duck, dug
Ed—Egg
Frank—Frankfurter
Fred—Fret
George—Gorge
Harold—Hair old
Howard—How art
James—Games
Jeff—Chef
John—Yawn
Ken—Can
Larry—Law (night stick)
Leonard—Lean hard
Mark—Mark, (Magic) Marker™
Michael—Microphone
Neil—Nail
Norman—Normal
Patrick—Pet trick

Paul—Ball
Phil—Fill, Phillips (screwdriver)
Ray—Ray gun
Richard—Dollars
Robert—Robber
Ron—Run
Roy—Soy (sauce)
Sam—Wham
Scott—Cot
Steven—Step on
Ted—Teddy bear
Terry—Terry cloth
Tim—Tin
Tom—Tom Tom (drums)
Vincent—Win cent
Walter—Wall tear

Women's First Names

Alice—Allen (wrench)
Ann—Ant
Barbara—Bra
Betty—Bet tees
Beverly—Bufferin™
Bonnie—Bonnet
Carmen—Carmel
Carol—Barrel
Cathy—Cat
Cheryl—Cherry
Chris—Crisco™, crisp
Cindy —Sin tee
Colleen—Call lean
Denise—Knees
Diane—Die ant
Doris—Lavoris™

Dorothy—Dot
Eileen—I lean
Ethel—Gasoline
Gwendolyn—Dwindlin'
Hazel—Hazelnut
Helen—Hell
Isabelle—Is a bell
Jane—Pain
Jean—Jeans
Jennifer—Gin and fur
Joan—Groan
Joanne—Chowin'
Joyce—Joy
Judy—Juice
Julie—Jewel
Karen—Carrying, caring
Kerry—Carry
Laura—Law (night stick)
Linda—Line
Lisa—Pizza
Margaret—Mark it
Marsha—Marshmallow
Mary—Marry
Maureen—More rain
Melissa—I'll miss her
Nancy—Antsy (nervous)
Pam—Bam
Patti—Pat
Peggy—Peck, pecking
Phyllis—Fill us
Sandi—Sandy
Susan—Sand
Tanya—Tan ya' (you)
Terri—Terry cloth

Quick Reference — Last Name Soundalikes

A

Abbott—A Boot
Abbruzese—I bruise easy
Abernathy—A bear nasty
Abrahamson—Ape ham sun
Abramowitz—Ape ram a witz (brains)
Abrams—Ape rams
Ackerman—Actor man
Adamchak—Atom jack, Atom check
Adams—Atoms, a dam
Adler—Add law (night stick hitting)
Aguillo—A wheel low
Ahearn—I learn
Aieello—Eye (in) Jello™
Albert—Prince Albert in a Can
Aldridge—All ridge, old ridge
Alexander—Axel land her, axel
Alfaro—All far o
Algozzini—All go see me
Allen—Allen (wrench), all in
Allessi—All I see
Almonte—All mount tee
Alpern—All burn
Alvarez—All for S (asp)
Amato—Tomato
Anderson—Ant ate son
Andrews—Ant rules (ruler)
Anthony—A toe knee
Argenio—Our jean's an o
Arruda—A root
Artley—Art (paint brush) leaks
Arvidson—R (hour) fits some
Ascot—Ass cot, S (asp) caught
Ashburn—Ash burn
Ashley—Ash leak
Askew—Ask ewe
Asperas—Asparagus, "Oh spare us!"
Attenasio—A tin I see o

B

Bacher—Back her
Bachman—Back man
Badash—Bad ash
Bailey—White bottle (the liqueur)
Bain—Pain
Baldwin—Bald win
Bannon—Pan in
Baranowski—Bear on a ski
Barclay—Bar clay
Barnett—Bar net
Barrett—Parrot
Barry—Berry
Bartlett—Pears
Barton—Bar tin
Baskin—Basking
Battelene—Bottle lean
Baxter—Bags stir
Baynes—Pains
Bazarnik—Bizarre nick
Beasley—Beastly
Beck—Peck
Beckley—Peck leak
Befumo—Perfume o
Begany—Beg a knee
Belvin—Bell fin
Belzer—Bells are
Bemmish—Blemish
Benaim—Pen name
Bennett—Pen net
Benoit—Pen hoit (hurt)
Berchtold—Birch (tree) told
Berrisano—Berries sand o
Bertino—Bird in o
Bertram—Bird ran, ram
Berustrom—Berries storm
Berman—Beer man
Bigelow—Big or low

Last Name Soundalikes Continued:

Blackiston—Black (shoe polish) a stone
Blaine—Plane
Blaisdell—Blaze a trail
Blake—Brake, lake
Blanchard—Branch yard
Blatt—Splatt
Blythe—Plight
Bochner—Block in there
Bock—Block
Bolden—Bolting, bolt in
Bonacci—Bone itchy
Boshar—Bow share
Bostick—Boss stick
Bourassa—Boraxo™
Bowman—Bow man
Boyd—Bird
Boyles—Boils
Brablec—Grab lick
Brady—Braids
Branson—Brand some
Bray—Pray
Brennan—Pen in
Brent—Dent
Brexell—Brakes L (Elf)
Brice—Price
Brill—Brillo pad™
Brindell—Pin (in a) dell
Briteheart—Bite heart
Brophy—Trophy
Bruner—Prune, prune her
Bryan—Iron
Bryant—Iron
Buckley—Buckle
Bullard—Bull yard
Burgon—Iceberg on
Burke—Iceberg
Buswell—Bus well, Buzz well
Buttrick—(Cigarette) butt trick

C

Calderon—Colt her on
Caldwell—Called well
Calero—Color
Callahan—Call a hand
Calter—Colt tear
Cameron—Camera on
Caminiti—Cam (engine) on a tee
Campbell—Soup
Cantero—Can't tear o
Cantrell—Can't trail
Caraway—Carry away
Carey—Carry
Carlile—Car isle
Carmody—Car muddy
Carnes—Cars
Carras—Carries
Carrington—Carry a ton
Carroll—Barrel
Carter—Car tear
Cassidy—Cast city
Cassin—Cast in
Castagna—Cast on ya'
Castenbotter—Cast in water
Castiglione—Castle alone
Castillo—Cast till o
Casto—Cast o
Cavanaugh—Half a knot
Cecil—Seesaw
Cerutti—Sear (burn) a tee
Chadwick—Chat candle (wick)
Chamblee—Jam bee
Chandler—Channel
Chaney—Chain E (eel)
Chapman—Chapstick™ man
Chaput—Shape it, stay put
Chernaault—Turn old
Chesler—Chiseler

Last Name Soundalikes Continued:

Chilton—Chill ton
Chonko—Chunk o
Chouinard—Shoe in yard
Christopher—Cross (Christ) of fur
Christopherson—Cross of fur from sun
Christopolus—Cross of Poles
Clancy—Chancy
Clark—Park
Claus—Claws
Clegg—Keg
Clifford—Cliff fort
Cloer—Lower
Cloutier—Cloudier
Cody—Coat tee
Cohen—(Ice cream) cone
Coletrain—Train carrying coal
Colletti—Call a tee
Collibus—Call a bus
Collier—Collar
Collins—Call n's (ants)
Conant—Cone ant
Connely—Corn will leave
Connor—Corner
Conover—Can of fur
Cooper—Chicken coop
Copeland—Coke land
Corbett—Corvette™
Coren—(Apple) Core in
Cornelio—Corn nail an o
Cortese—Cord tease
Coverdale—Cover tail
Coviello—Cove in Jello™
Crawford—Claw ford
Creedon—Cretin
Crenshaw—Can of chaw (tobacco)
Cromwell—Crumb well
Cronk—Conk
Crosby—Cross bee
Crystalowicz—Crystal O' witz (brains)

Cullen—Color in
Culotta—S' (it's) a lotta
Culpepper—Coal pepper
Culver—Cover
Cunningham—Cutting ham
Curceo—Curse and O' (cherrio)
Curran—Car run
Curtis—Curt S (asp)
Cusimano—Cuss a mean o

D

Dale—Tail
Dalessio—Tail is an o
Dalloway—Fall away
Dalton—Doll ton
Danforth—Den forth
Daniels—Tan L's (elves)
Dannatt—Tan it
Dante—Dent a (ape)
Danzinger—Dance injure
Darman—Tar man
Darsch—Harsh
Darvin—Tar fin
Davenport—Dove in port
Davidoff—(Star of) David (falling) off
Davis—Save us
Dawson—Doors on
De fluri—(Golf) tee flurry, floor E (eel)
Dean—Lean
Degress—Tee in grass
Degruccio—Tee grouchy o
Deguzman—Tee cuss man
Dektor—Doctor, deck tore
Del Gaizo—Dell gaze an o
Delaney—(Golf) tee lane E (eel)
Dembski—Dumb ski
Denton—Dent in
Dershimer—Dish em' more

Last Name Soundalikes Continued:

Desantis—(Golf) tee sand
Desmond—Dice mound
Desnoyer—Deny her
Devaney—(Golf) tee is vaney
Delvin—Devil in
Di Atillio—(Golf) tee tilling o
Di Bello—Tee bell o
Diefenbach—Deaf in back
Digby—Dig bee
Dinzik—Tin sick
Dodson—Dots sun
Doetzer—Dots her
Dole—Pineapple
Donato—Donut toe
Donelan—Funnel in
Donovan—Run a van
Dooley—Duelling
Doran—Door ran
Dougherty—Dirty
Douglas—Dug glass
Doyle—Boil
Dozier—Bulldozer
Drachenberg—Drag a (ice)berg
Drysdale—Dry tail
Dubinsky—Two pins ski
Duffin—Stuffin'
Duffy—Tuffy
Dulski—Dull ski
Duncan—Dunk can, dunk in
Dunlap—Done lap (finished a lap)
Dunzik—Done (being) sick
Durant—Door ran
Dutton—Button
Duvall—Dew fall
Dwyer—Dryer

E

Ebersole—Ever sold
Eble—Able
Eckerdt—Egg hurt
Eckler—Heckler
Edberg—Egg (ice)berg
Edelin—Eat a line
Edmondson—Egg mound sun
Edwards—Egg warts
Egusquiza—A goose keys ya
Eide—Hide
Eikel—I kill
Elias—He lies
Elliot—'Ell e's odd
Ellrich—L (elf) rich
Elmquist—Elm kissed
Emley—M (M&M™) leak
Engle—Angle
Erno—Urn o
Espinet—S (asp) pin net
Esposito—S (asp) pole sit o
Estes—S (asp) (golf) tees
Etterly—Et' (ate) a leaf
Evans—Even
Everitt—Half of it

F

Faber—Paper
Fagan—Fakin', Ray gun
Falasco—Flask o
Farnoff—Far off
Farolino—Far a lean o
Farrell—Barrel
Faubus—Foe bus
Faucher—Pouch her
Fay—Hay
Fazenbaker—Fuzz n' baker

Last Name Soundalikes Continued:

Fealey—Fig leaf
Fedderson—Fed the sun
Federico—Fed a reek (ing) o
Feldman—Felt man (man made of felt)
Felton—Felt ton (ton made of felt)
Fenton—Dent in
Ferguson—Fur cuss son
Fernandez—Firm hand is
Ferrier—Furrier
Fetter—Fed her
Fichtner—Fit her
Fiedor—Feed a door
Finney—Penny
Finnigan—Win again
Firth—First
Fitzgerald—Fits a cherry
Fitzsimmons—Fits wins one
Fixel—Fix L (Elf)
Flah—Blah
Flanigan—Flame again
Flannery—Flattery
Fletcher—Letch
Floyd—Flight
Flynn—Flint
Fogleman—Vocal man
Fogt—Vote
Foley—Folly
Foltz—Folds
Foran—Forehand
Fortini—Fort teeny
Forzano—Force an o
Foster—Force tear
Fowler—Flower
Frager—Faker
Frankel—Frank (hot dog) L (elf)
Frank—Hot dog
Frasca—Fresca™
Frazier—Razor
Frechette—Fresh et' (ate)

Friedhopfer—Freed hopper
Friedlander—Freed land

G

Gallbraith—Call breath
Galeta—Call it at
Gallagher—Call a fur
Gallahan—Call a hand
Gampolo—Game of polo
Garcia—(Ci) gar see ya'
Garrison—Carry the sun
Garrity—Carrot key
Garrott—Carrot
Gartner—Garter
Gaultney—Cold knee
Gelman—Kill man
Gennett—Can it
Gentin—Bent in
Gerber—Baby food
Giagregorio—Gin in cracked car
Gibson—(Vodka) Gibson
Gilbert—Kill bird
Gillis—Kill us
Gingras—Gin grass
Ginocchio—Pinocchio
Girten—Hurtin'
Giscard—Discard
Giuliano—Jewel in an o
Glick—Click
Golinski—Coal on ski
Gomez—Go mess, combs
Gonzales—Gone (to get) salve
Goodner—Good in there
Gordon—Garden
Gorenkoff—(Apple) Core in cough
Gorgens—Gorge n's (ants)
Gorman—(Apple) Core man
Gosiminski—Go see mints ski

Last Name Soundalikes Continued:

Goulet—Goo lay
Gove—Glove, dove
Grabler—Grab her
Grabowski—Grab a ski
Grady—Grading
Graham—Cracker
Granato—Cram a toe
Gravett—Grab it
Gregory—Keg or key
Grigsby—Grabs bee
Grogan—Grow gun
Grover—Grow fur
Guerrero—Career o
Guinn—Win
Gulliver—Gull (made) of fur
Gunther—Gun tear
Gustafson—Cuss the sun
Guthrie—Cut tree

H

Haferkamp—Half a camp
Hagen—Hackin'
Haggerty—Hack a tee
Haley—Comet
Halloran—Hollering
Hamilton—Ham a ton
Hamlin—Ham line (line of ham)
Hamner—Hammer
Hamzik—Ham sick
Hanley—Hand leak
Hannah—Hand her
Hannifan—Hand a fan
Hanson—Handsome
Harackiewicz—Hairy carrots
Hardesty—Hard as (a cup of) tea
Harnagel—Hard bagel
Harper—Harp
Harrington—Herring ton

Harris—Hairless
Hartigan—Heart again
Hartley—Heart leak (ly)
Hartnett—Hard net
Hawes—Horse
Healey—Healing
Hebrank—He brake
Hedberg—Head (Ice) berg
Hefler—Half law
Heinz—Ketchup
Heiser—Hi sore
Helms—Helm
Henderson—Hand her some
Hendricks—Hen tricks
Hennessey—Hens see
Hernandez—Firm hand is
Herron—Blue heron
Hersberger—Hurts a berger
Hersch—Candy bar
Herschfield—Field of candy bars
Hettinger—Head injure
Hicks—Sticks
Hignite—Ignite
Hilderbrandt—Hills of bran
Hiltz—Hills
Hines—Ketchup
Hintz—Hints
Hoagland—Hoagie (sandwich) on land
Hobbs—Hops
Hodge—Dodge
Hoffman—Huff man
Hogan—Hoe gun
Holcomb—Whole comb
Hollis—Holes
Holmes—Homes
Holt—Hold
Holtzwasser—Holes, holds water
Holway—Hallway
Holzberg—Holes in (ice)berg

Last Name Soundalikes Continued:

Holzshu—Hold shoe, whole shoe
Honeycutt—Honey cut
Hoover—Vacuum cleaner
Hosmer—Hot smear
Howell—Howl, how will?
Hugel—Ewe kill
Hughes—Use
Hurley—Hurling
Hutchinson—Huts in sun
Hyatt—Buy it

I

Iacovello—Yak a bell (cheeri) o
Ian—E (eel) in
Ingerbritzon—Ink her bit some
Inman—In man
Irwin—Fur win
Israel—Star of David
Issacs—Eye is sick

J

Jackson—Jacks in
Jacobs—J (Bluejay) cups
Jacobus—Jack a bus
Jaffe—Chafing
Jagowicz—Jacks or witz
Jankalow—Yank it low
Jarrett—Jar it
Jarski—Jar ski
Jarvic—Jar fit
Jasin—Chasin'
Jeeter—Cheater
Jensen—Jam some
Jerome—Chair roam
Jessop—Chess up
Jordan—Garden of jars
Joseph—Aspirin (St. Josephs™)

K

Kahlert—Alert
Kahn—Snobby can
Kairella—Cruller donuts
Kaiser—Roll
Kakish—Cactus
Kallett—Ballet
Kantor—Can tore, Cantor
Kaplan—Cap land
Kardis—Card is
Karlin—Car line
Keating—Cheating
Keegan—Key in
Keelor—Key law
Keller—Killer
Kelly—Kill E (eel)
Kemper—Camper
Kennedy—Can of tees (D's)
Kenyon—Canyon
Keoski—Key or ski
Kerner—Burner
Kerr—Furr
Kessler—Kiss her
Kileen—Clean
Kilpatrick—Kill that trick
Kinchen—Kitchen
Kinsey—Can see
Kippenberger—Kept a burger
Kirk—Hurt
Kirkpatrick—Hurt that trick
Kliban—Climb on
Knackstedt—Nap Step
Koenig—Cone nick
Kilodny—Clot knee
Kosloff—Gauze off
Kosloski—Gauze lost key
Kosovsky—Gauze off ski
Kotecki—Coat tacky

Last Name Soundalikes Continued:

Kottich—Coat itch
Kovacs—Go back
Kramer—Creamer
Kreer—Career
Kritch—Itch
Kuhn—(Rac) coon
Kurlander—Curl land her
Kushnirak—Cushion rack

L

Lally—Lolly (pop)
Lamonica—Harmonica
Lange—Lank
Larson—Lost sun
Laskin—Less skin
Laughran—Laugh rap
Laventhol—Lather all
Lawrence—Law (night stick) rents
            (house)
Lazaroff—Laser (gun) off
Lederman—Letter man
Lee—Leak
Leighton—Lay ton
Lenson—Lend some
Leone—Lean on me
Leonhardt—Lean hard
Lerham—Fur ham
Lester—Less tear
Levine—Ravine
Levitt—Leave it
Levy—Jeans
Lewis—Loose
Lieberman—Leaf a man
Liedtke—Lead key
Lindsay—Lindseed
Lindstrom—Lint strum
Lippet—Lip it
Lo Brutto—Low brute

Logan—Low gun
Loomis—Loom
Lopez—Low fez
Loring—Law (night stick) ink
Losyk—Low sick
Lubinski—Lube in ski
Lucas—Look kiss
Ludwig—Lead wig
Lundberg—Lunge (ice) berg
Lutz—Klutz
Lybrand—Lie brand

M

MacGowan—My cow in
MacMurray—My hurry
Macaluso—Mack (truck) a loose o
Macchiarella—Match a real
Madden—Mad den
Maginn—Mack (truck) in
Maguire—My wire
Magyar—Mag (azine) in yard
Mahoney—Baloney
Malandro—Mail and grow
Malconian—Mail a cone in ant
Malinowski—Mail on a ski
Malinox—Mail knock
Malone—Alone
Malooley—My loose leaf
Maltese—Malt tease, falcon
Mancuso—Man curse o
Manning—Man ink
Manniyar—Many yards
Marconi—Macaroni
Marcott—My cot
Marcus—Mark us
Marello—My real o
Marguin—Marking
Marino—Marine o

Last Name Soundalikes Continued:

Markevich—Mark a witch
Marko—Mark o
Markowitz—Mark a brain (witz)
Martin—My tin
Maseley—Maze leak
Massey—Messy
Mathis—Mattress
Matsuda—Mat suit
Matthews—Mat use
Maurice—More rice
Mauser—Mouse
Maxwell—Coffee can
Mayer—Mayor
Mazor—Razor
Mcanlis—My candles
McCabe—My cape
McCarthy—Mack (truck) car tee
McCarty—Mack (truck) car tee
McConville—My con fill
McCoy—My coy
McDonald—Mack Donald (duck)
McDowell—My towel
McFarland—Mack far land
McGarvey—My (ci) gar v (veal)
McGavin—My cabin
McGee—My key
McGill—My gill, my kill
McGuigan—My wick in
McGuirk—My quirk
McIntire—Mack (truck) in tire
McKenna—My camera
McKernan—My fur in
McMahel—My mail
McPherson—My fierce sun
Medford—Met ford
Meehan—Me hand
Meese—Mice
Meinhard—Mine hard
Melville—Mail fill

Meno—Mean o
Merwin—Fur win
Metcalf—Met calf
Michaels—Mike (microphone) kills
Middleton—Middle ton
Minton—Mitten
Mitchell—Miss hell
Monek—More neck
Monroe—One row
Montgomery—Mount of gum
Montrone—Monotone
Morales—Morals
Moran—More run
Morgan—More gun
Morris—Morse (code)
Morrison—Morse (code) sun
Morrissey—More sea
Morton—Salt
Moskal—Moss kill
Mostad—Mustard
Moyle—Boil
Mueller—Mule her
Mullins—Mole in
Mundy—Moon tea
Murphy—More peas
Murrell—Mural

N

Nagel—Bagel
Naismith—Neigh smith (hammer)
Nash—Gnash, mash
Navarro—No far o
Navetta—No feta (cheese)
Naylor—Tailor, nail her
Nayo—Mayo
Nedells—Needles
Neff—Enough
Nelson—Nails in

Last Name Soundalikes Continued:

Nesbitt—Nice bit
Nesenoff—Messing off
Newton—Fig Newton™ cookie,
       new ton
Nieto—Knee a toe
Nittolo—Knit all o
Nixon—Nicks on
Nobile—No bile
Nolette—No (don't) let
Norbeck—Door peck
Norsworthy—Newsworthy
North—Compass
Norwood—No wood
Noyce—Noise
Nugent—Nugget

O

O'Brien—(Cheeri) O crying
O'Connor—O corner
O'Keefe—O keys
O'Neil—O nail
O'Reilley—O really?
Ogden—Ug(ly) den
Oglivie—Ogle bee
Oliver—Olive fur
Olson—Old sun
Oppenheim—Open I'm
Oprehezen—Opera hazing
Orben—Or pen
Ortis—Oar tears
Osmond—O's (on a) mound
Osterland—O's steer land
Ostrout—O's strut
Ouley—Oak leaf, leak
Owens—O wins

P

Paley—Pale leak
Palmer—Palm her
Passarell—Pass a bell
Patterson—Pat the sun
Pauley—Ball leak
Pearce—Pierce, Pears
Peckham—Peck ham
Pegram—Peg ram
Pelletier—Pellet tear
Peppler—Pepper
Perez—Pez
Perkins—Perking
Perlmutter—Pearl mutter
Perlov—Pearl off
Petrozelli—Pat rose sell E (eel)
Phillips—Screwdriver
Pilla—Pillow
Pimentel—Pimento
Pisonero—Peas on arrow
Placek—Play check
Plourde—Plowed
Polhemos—Pull lame o's
Pollack—Pole lack
Poncy—Bouncy
Popovich—Pop a fist
Porfideo—Pour video
Posluszny—Poles lost knee
Poulos—Poles
Powell—Towel
Pringle—Potato chips
Pritchard—Pitch hard
Prizzio—Pretty (Cheeri) o
Provenzano—Pro van's an o
Provost—Pro post
Pullano—Pull an o
Purtle—Turtle
Putnal—Put nail

Last Name Soundalikes Continued:

Q

Quairtius—Quarter us, S (asp)
Quattelbaum—Bottle bomb
Quigley—Wiggly
Quinlan—Win one
Quinn—Win
Quisenberry—Squeezin' berry

R

Radigan—Rat again
Radziwill—Rats in well
Rafferty—Laugh a tee
Ragali—Rag gully
Raguz—Spaghetti sauce
Raguzzo—Rag goo sew
Raleigh—Roll E (eel)
Rampell—Ramp bell
Randall—Ran doll
Rapkin—Napkin
Rathbun—Rash bun
Ratney—Rat knee
Raziano—Razz an o
Reardon—Rear den
Reark—Real ark
Reddecliff—Ready cliff
Redinger—Read injure
Reeves—Leaves
Reichley—Wright leak
Reinhardt—Write hard
Rejko—Let go
Relkenis—Real tennis
Resnick—Rest nick
Reynolds—Rain old, aluminum foil
Richardson—Rich (dollars) from the sun
Richter—Rick (of wood) tear, tricked her
Riggio—Itchy o
Riggs—Ricks (wood)

Riley—Wiley
Rittenhouse—White on house
Robertson—Robber son
Roby—Robe
Rodrique—(Fishing) rod reeks
Rojas—Row ha!
Rollins—Roll ants (n's)
Rondeau—Run doe
Ross—Floss
Rostock—Rust stuck
Roth—Rot
Rothstein—Rot cup
Rosseau—Lasso, you sew
Rubin—Sandwich
Rutherford—Roquefort
Ryan—Iron
Ryker—Rye fur

S

Sabbatini—Sap is teeny
Sabinyerzi—Sap in fur see
Sadovnick—Sad of nick
Sala—Salad
Samuels—Animals
Sanchez—Sand chase
Sanders—Sand
Sanderson—Sand her some
Sannicandro—Sunny can grow
Santoriello—Sand tore the jello
Santoro—Sand tore o
Santos—Sand toes, sand toast
Santulli—Sand pulley
Sawyer—Saw
Saxon—Sax (aphone) on
Scadlock—Scat lock, bad luck
Scala—Scald a
Scalise—Scale lease
Schaeffer—Shaver

Last Name Soundalikes Continued:

Schefter—Shift her
Scheibe—Shy bee
Schinmann—Shin man
Schleicher—Like her
Schlossberg—Shlossed (drunk) berg
Schlosser—Shlosser (more drunk)
Schmidt—(Blacksmith's) hammer
Schneider—Sly door
Schoenholt—Show and hold
Schrader—Shredder
Schroeder—Wrote her
Schultz—Schlitz™
Schuppert—Sherbert
Schuster—Shoe stir, shoe store
Schwab—Q-tip™
Schwartz—Warts
Sculley—Skull
Sears—Burn
Sebok—Reebok™ (sneakers)
Selvig—Sell fig
Senkarik—Send carrot
Sepanik—Don't panic
Sercia—Search for her
Shaughnessy—Sure messy
Shaw—Chaw (chewing tobacco)
Shay—Shade
Sheehan—She hand
Shelton—Shell ton, skeleton
Sherman—Share man
Sherriton—Share a ton
Shupe—Chute, shoot
Siegel—Seagull
Silber—Silver
Simon—Dime in
Simpson—Simp (le) son
Sitron—Sit run
Skidmore—Skid more
Slade—Slate
Slifer—Slicer

Sloan—Loan, groan
Slocum—Slow comb
Smith—(Blacksmith's) hammer
Sneed—Sneeze
Snyder—Shy door
Sobotka—Sew vodka
Solomon—Salmon
Solson—Sole sun
Sommers—Summers
Sooker—Sucker
Sorvino—Sore wine (vino)
Sosa—Sews a
Spagnola—Smack no la (music)
Spector—Spec (eyeglass) tore
Spence—Coin
Squire—Wire
Starling—Star ink, darling
Staub—Stab
Steckhan—Stick ham
Stephens—Step on
Stern—Strict
Stevenson—Step on sun
Stewart—(Beef) stew, paintbrush (art)
Stinson—Stand sun
Stratton—Struttin', strap on
Strauss—Mouse
Stroud—Loud
Sullivan—Sell a van
Suprun—Soup run
Sutcliffe—Sat cliff
Sveen—Screen
Swanson—Swan sun
Swaroop—Swear rope
Sweeney—Sweetly

Last Name Soundalikes Continued:

T

Tandon—Tandem
Tarricone—Tear a cone
Tarsches—Tar is
Tassani—Too sunny
Tate—Date
Taub—Tub
Teasley—Tease leak
Tebodo—Tea bow doe
Teft—Tough
Teitelbaum—Title bomb
Telsey—Tell see
Tenzer—Tin stir
Terrasconi—Terrace cone
Terry—Terry cloth
Thatcher—Catcher
Thayer—They are
Theriault—Terry (cloth) old
Thibodeau—Tip a doe
Thomas—Thumbs
Thompson—Thumbs sun
Thon—Thorn
Tinsley—Tins leak
Tirshel—Turn shell
Tobias—Toe buy us
Toney—Toe knee
Topham—Top ham
Towner—Town
Townsend—Town send
Trammel—Trample
Travers—Travels
Travis—Travel
Trebowski—Trip ow ski
Trujillo—True hill o
Tuttle—Turtle
Tyler—Tie

U

Udell—Ewe tell
Unger—Hunger
Uschman—Hush, man!
Utley—Hut leak

V

Vadnais—Bad day
Vaillancourt—Fell in court
Van Vliet—Van fleet
Vanacore—Van a core (apple)
Vandenberg—Van den berg
Vaneecke—Van "eek!"
Vanhoy—Van toy
Vantrease—Van trees
Vaughan—Fawn
Veglia—Fig leaf
Venable—Fan a bull
Venzara—Fan saw her
Verhey—Fur he
Verity—Ferret tea
Vesper—Whisper
Victor—Victory
Villaescusa—We'll excuse ya'
Vincent—Win cent
Vinho—Vino (wine)
Vining—Vine ink
Vlach—Latch
Vogel—Ogle
Volz—Volts
Voss—Floss

Last Name Soundalikes Continued:

W

Wagner—Wagging her
Walesky—Wall list ski
Wallace—Wall lace, lock
Walsh—Wash
Walters—Wall tears
Ward—Wart
Warner—Warn her
Warren—Worn
Washam—Wash ham
Watkins—Watt (light bulb) cans
Watson—Watt (light bulb) in
Watts—Watt (light bulb)
Waverly—Wave
Weber—Web bear
Webster—Web stir, dictionary
Wedderburn—Wet a burn
Weintraub—Wine a trout
Weiss—Wise (owl)
Wellington—Well ink ton
Wenderoth—Went to rot
Wengatz—Win gates
Wenzel—Pencil
Werbalowsky—Wear a low ski
Whalen—Wailing
Whaley—Whale
Whitkov—White (out) cove
Whitney—White (out) knee
Whitworth—White (out) worth
Wilcox—Will (fighting) cocks
Wilhelm—Will helm
Wilkerson—Wilt the sun
Williams—Yams
Wilson—Will sun
Windslow—Winds low
Wirtz—Hurts
Wisweell—Wish well

Withrow—Will throw, row
Wodraska—Would ask her
Woolsey—Wool sea
Worthington—Worth a ton
Wycoff—Why cough?

Y

Yambert—Yam bird
Yarbrough—Yard pro
Yarnell—Yard nail
Yerchin—Your chin
Yoder—Yodel
Yoho—Yo-yo

Z

Zadvinskis—Sand fin skis
Zakon—Sack on
Zaloom—Balloon
Zarkin—Parkin'
Zenda—Send her
Zimmer—Simmer
Zoeller—Seller
Zukowski—Zoo cow ski
Zullo—Too low

C HAPTER 5

English Vocabulary

An excellent vocabulary quite often distinguishes a successful person from an average one. One might think it shouldn't be so, but as with many things in life, it is. A person with a strong vocabulary is looked up to, respected, and most importantly, perceived to be smarter than he or she may actually be (sort of like the person with a great memory).

In his classic audio cassette program entitled *Lead The Field*, the late Earl Nightingale stresses the importance of a strong knowledge of one's native language. The results of several surveys in that area dramatically illustrate the fact that the better a person's vocabulary, the greater the chance that person has of succeeding in business...and vice versa.

Mr. Nightingale referred to an article by Blake Clark published in *Reader's Digest* which pointed out that "Tests of more than 350,000 persons from all walks of life show that more often than any other measurable characteristic, knowledge of the exact meanings of a large number of words accompanies outstanding success."

Another survey, according to Mr. Nightingale, revealed the following. "Many years ago the graduating class of a large university was given an examination in English Vocabulary. The test scores were graded into groups of 5% each: the top 5% and so on to the bottom. At regular intervals during the next 20 years, questionnaires were sent to the surviving graduates asking them their occupations, incomes and so on. Without a single exception, those who scored highest on the vocabulary test were in the top income group, while those who scored lowest were in the lowest income group." Isn't that fascinating?

Referring back to the article by Mr. Blake in *Reader's Digest*, Mr. Nightingale related the results of a study by scientist Johnson O'Connor. The study vividly illustrated the fact that with all basic aptitudes relating to leadership being equal among executive and supervisory personnel in 39 large manufacturing plants, a strong vocabulary was the *only* significant (and definite!) difference between company presidents and vice-presidents and those on the lowest levels of management.

The ability to quickly improve your vocabulary can therefore be a truly profitable attribute, and the techniques in this chapter will start you well on your way toward that goal. Incidentally, there are many ways to enrich your vocabulary, but I truly believe the method that follows is the simplest and quickest way to achieve a significant improvement.

This method will use the same basic memory technique of association, the joining together of two items, one you already know with another you wish to remember. It will also employ the use of the Soundalike. Let's first look at a couple of examples.

Mitigate means to soften. In order to learn that, we would need to find a way to associate the two. But of course the word *mitigate* by itself is intangible. So let's use a Soundalike word or phrase for mitigate that we can see. How about *mitt a gate*? Can't you just picture a mitt, or mitten, on a gate? Your natural memory will tell you that mitt is really a mitten. Associating "mitt a gate" with "soften" will be a lot easier, won't it? After all, if you put a mitten on a gate, wouldn't it definitely soften that part of the gate? That is how it is done. My Soundalike, *mitt a gate*, works for me, but you might use something else. Possibly *mud on gate* or *mad at gate*, or you may have pictured the mitt in "mitt a gate" being a baseball mitt.

Let's walk through another example. The word *olfactory* pertains to the sense of smell. First, let's take the word *olfactory,* which by itself doesn't present a picture, and turn it into something that does. The Soundalike *old factory* will work, won't it? I would suggest picturing yourself walking through a very old factory and realizing that it smells real bad.

Simple enough, isn't it? The good news is that it will work for virtually any word. The bad news is that they are not all quite that easy. In fact, you will really have to play with many of them in order to make them work. The key word in that last sentence, however, is *play*. Please make it fun for yourself. You will get a kick out of realizing just how fast you can improve your ability to learn new words.

The words will be set up as follows. First, the word we want to learn. In parentheses, the Soundalike word or phrase I suggest (very loosely suggest, since you know that your own Soundalike, if different from mine, will work better for you). Then, one definition of the word; possibly more if they are similar in meaning and easier to explain that way. And finally, a suggestion on how to put it all together in order to remember it. Every so often, look back and review the words and their definitions.

Ratification (rat a vacation)—*approval; sanction; confirmation.* You want to give a rat a vacation. You undoubtedly have his approval.

Captious (capture us)—*disposed to find fault or raise objection.* If you capture us, I will definitely find fault with that and object.

Faux pas—pronounced foe paw (foe paw)—*a social blunder.* When your foe raised his paw to you in public, that was a social blunder.

Hippodrome (hippo dome)—*an arena or building for a circus, games, etc.* Picture a building in the shape of a dome. Inside is a gigantic circus hippo(potamus.)

Neophyte (new fight)—*a novice.* That novice is so new, he is not ready to fight.

Vacillate (Vaseline™)—*to waver; show indecision.* You are wavering and are indecisive as to whether you should use Vaseline™.

Piteous (pity us)—*sad; wretched; sorrowful.* Pity us because we are so sad.

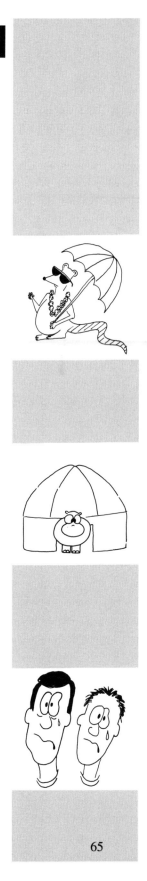

Ablution (add lotion)—*the washing of the body as preparation for religious duties*. A good way to wash the body as preparation for religious duties is to add lotion.

Kismet (kiss me)—*fate*. Say to your mate, "My dear, it was fate that you decided to kiss me."

Ribald (rye bald)—*characterized by coarse joking or mocking*. Picture a piece of rye bread having a mocking type of humor and telling coarse jokes.

Machinate (machine ate)—*to plot, especially with evil intent*. A machine ate all the files, and plotted to do it with evil intent.

Stultify (stilt defy)—*to cause to appear foolish*. Wearing stilts in order to defy society would probably cause one to appear foolish.

Ubiquitous (you bigger us)—*existing everywhere*. You are so much bigger than us, it seems as though you exist everywhere.

Babushka (bush)—*a kerchief or scarf*. Picture a gigantic kerchief or scarf covering a bush.

Irascible (erasable)—*irritable; easily provoked to anger*. If a person were erasable, she would probably be very irritable.

Supercilious (super silly)—*arrogant; overbearing*. That person was not only super silly, but arrogant and overbearing as well.

Poniard (pony yard)—*a small dagger*. Picture a pony in a yard. It has a small dagger between its teeth.

Nabob (neigh Bob)—*a wealthy person*. Picture a very wealthy guy named Bob being spoken to by his horse. (Get it?) All right, bad one.

Temperance (temper ants)—*moderation*. What a bad temper on those ants! They ought to try to at least keep it in moderation.

Accouchement (a couch mint)—*birth*. Picture a human mint on a couch. She has just given birth to a baby mint.

Discordant (this cord ant)—*disagreeing; contradictory.* Both ants want this cord. They are disagreeing on who should have it.

Noxious (obnoxious)—*harmful to health or morals.* Imagine that people who are obnoxious can be harmful to health or morals.

Seditious (sad dishes)—*having a tendency to rebel.* You can imagine that sad dishes have a tendency to rebel against being washed in dishwater.

Punchinello (punchin' Jello)—*a buffoon.* This one pretty much explains itself, doesn't it?

Litany (lit a knee)—*a form of prayer.* Imagine you lit your knee. Then you said a prayer over it.

Indolent (in Dole™ ant)—*habitually idle; lazy.* Back to those ants. This one is inside a Dole™ pineapple. It is both idle and lazy.

Garrulity (car pull a tee)—*talkativeness.* Picture a car pulling a gigantic golf tee. They are talking the entire time.

Antecede (Aunty seed)—*to go before in place, order, or time.* Everyone planted seeds, but Aunty got to go before anyone else.

Decorous (decorate)—*showing good taste; proper.* They decorated the room in very good taste.

Milquetoast (milk toast)—*a timid, shrinking, apologetic type person.* Make believe that people who fit this definition always drink milk with their toast.

Rhapsody (rap city)—*an instrumental composition of free, irregular form, suggesting improvisation.* Picture a bunch of people rapping with each other in the city. They are rapping about the idea of putting together an instrumental composition, and doing a lot of improvising.

Bumptious (bumps us)—*conceited; self-assertive.* She bumps into us all the time because she is very conceited and self-assertive.

Falderal (fault at all)—*a trifle; mere nonsense*. You think that it was her fault at all? That is mere nonsense.

Misnomer (misname)—*to misname*. This is one of those which just happens to work out perfectly.

Sedulous (schedule us)—*constant; steady and persevering*. You can schedule us with confidence because we are constant and steady.

Eradicate (rat a gate)—*to destroy at the roots; to wipe out*. Picture a gigantic rat at a gate. He destroys the gate right from its roots and wipes out the entire gate.

Benediction (Benny diction)—*an invocation of divine blessing, which usually follows a ceremony*. Picture someone you know named Benny showing good diction while giving an invocation.

Peduncle (pet uncle)—*a flower stalk*. You give your favorite (pet) uncle a flower stalk.

Arrogate (arrow gate)—*to claim, demand, or seize unduly*. Imagine yourself shooting an arrow into a gate, then claiming that gate as your own.

Lodestar (lead star)—*a star by which one directs his/her course*. Picture one of these stars up in the sky being your lead star; the star by which you direct your course.

Wont (want)—*custom; habit*. You want to keep doing the same thing because it has become a custom or habit.

Citadel (city dell)—*stronghold; a refuge*. See an entire city built in a dell (valley) being your refuge.

Ethereal (ether real)—*very light; airy; heavenly*. After sniffing real ether, things get very light and airy.

Laggard (lag)—*slow; sluggish*. Having jet lag can make you feel slow and sluggish.

Hackneyed (hack knee)—*made commonplace by overuse*. Imagine that you hacked at somebody's knee so much, that knee became very commonplace.

Jocund (jock)—*merry; genial; cheerful.* Picture a jock (athlete) who is very cheerful.

Elucidate (lose a date)—*to explain.* If you lose a date while out with that person, you'd better be able to explain what happened.

Gaucherie (gouge an eye)—*tactlessness.* Wouldn't it be quite tactless to just gouge someone in the eye?

Unyoke (yolk)—*to separate or disconnect.* Picture yourself cracking open an egg, then separating the yolk from the white.

Plutocrat (Pluto)—*any wealthy person.* Imagine Mickey Mouse's dog, Pluto, being extremely wealthy.

Magnate (magnet)—*a very important or influential person in any field or activity.* Imagine a magnet being very important or influential.

Glabrous (glamorous)—*smooth; having no hair, down, or fuzz.* See a smooth, hairless celebrity being glamorous.

Superfluous (super floss)—*surplus.* It's super to floss your teeth because there happens to be a surplus of dental floss.

Paladin (pal)—*a heroic champion.* That heroic champion is my pal.

Bellwether (bell weather)—*the leader of a sheeplike crowd of followers.* Picture a bell, in bad weather, leading a sheeplike crowd of followers.

Lambent (lamp bent)—*flickering.* The lamp was bent so badly that its light would merely flicker.

Abyss (a bus)—*a bottomless pit.* See a bus falling into a bottomless pit.

Ostracize (ostrich size)—*to cast out or banish; to exclude.* The ostrich was so much larger than the regular size, she was banished from her group and totally excluded.

Raconteur (racketeer)—*one given to telling anecdotes.* Imagine an old-time racketeer sitting around telling anecdotes of the good ol' days.

Vestibule (vest a bull)—*a small entrance hall to a building.* Picture a bull, wearing a vest, trying to crash through a small entrance hall to a building.

Usurp (you syrup)—*to take and hold in possession by force without a right.* You took my syrup from me without the right to do so.

Placard (play card)—*a notice posted in a public place.* Take a gigantic play card (whatever that is) and post it as a notice in a public place.

Jerrybuilt (Jerry built)—*flimsy; built hurriedly and of inferior materials.* Picture someone named Jerry hurriedly building something flimsy out of inferior materials.

Umbrage (hmm, bridge)—*resentment; displeasure.* Hmm, I am very dissatisfied with the way they built that bridge.

Comestible (comb edible)—*food.* Picture a comb that is edible being your food.

Fetter (feather)—*to shackle or confine the feet with a chain.* Imagine shackling someone's feet with a chain, then taking a feather and tickling their feet.

Insipid (sip it)—*tasteless; flat; dull.* After you sipped it, you decided it was tasteless, flat and dull.

Skulduggery (skull dug)—*mean, contemptible actions; plotting.* A skull was dug out of the ground. That was a mean, contemptible action.

Opiate (Opie ate)—*that which induces rest.* Remember Opie from "The Andy Griffith Show"? Imagine he ate something that made him sleepy.

Veracity (fair city)—*truthfulness; honesty.* The reason we have such a fair city is because it was built on truthfulness and honesty.

Truculent (truck you lent)—*fierce; cruel; belligerent.* That truck you lent me ran me over. It was fierce, cruel and belligerent.

Tocsin (toxin)—*any warning signal.* If something is a toxin it should definitely have a warning signal right on it.

Infidel (in fiddle)—*not believing in any religion.* Imagine a person who does not believe in any religion, but in a fiddle instead.

Exculpate (eggs cold plate)—*to declare or prove guiltless.* Did the eggs take the cold plate? No, they were proven and declared guiltless.

Crestfallen (crest fallen)—*dejected; dispirited.* Imagine a tube of Crest™ toothpaste has fallen off the sink. Poor thing! It is dejected and dispirited.

Onerous (honor us)—*burdensome; laborious.* They gave us tasks that were burdensome and laborious. Is that any way to honor us?

Machiavellian (macho)—*unscrupulous; scheming; deceitful.* Do you know any macho guys who fit that description?

Vacuous (vacuum)—*empty; void.* After the vacuum got through cleaning the room, it seemed empty.

Conveyance (conveyor belt)—*transference; transportation.* It is easy to transfer something on a conveyor belt.

Fabricate (fabric)—*to construct, devise falsely.* Imagine someone cheating in order to construct a building out of fabric.

Atrophy (a trophy)—*to physically waste away.* Picture a trophy being so old that it begins to physically waste away.

See what can be accomplished by using just a bit of imagination? I'm not going to quiz you by giving you the words and asking you to write the definitions, or vice versa (yes, this will also work both ways). But I will ask that you review these words several times. In a very short period of time they will become true memory, and you won't need the associations. The difference between the above examples and many of those in other chapters (such as the made-up addresses or telephone numbers) is that you might actually need to know these particular words. So even though it was just another drill, it is information that could come in very handy. Of course, the more you practice with new words, the better you will become at using this technique.

Foreign Language Vocabulary

An ever-changing world—including an increase in immigration, travel and international business—has made it more and more advantageous to be adequate, if not fluent, in at least one other language besides English. This is not only to increase your chances of getting *ahead* in the business world, but also just to be able to keep up with the Joneses...or perhaps even the Nakamuras.

The aim of this chapter is not to teach you how to learn a foreign language. "What then is the point, Bob?" you might be asking. Good question. Let me explain.

By and large, the only way to become fluent in a foreign language is to immerse yourself in it to the point that it becomes *part of you*, and you are eventually able to think in that language. You no longer have to translate word-for-word, or idea-for-idea; you just know it.

It can, however, be considerably easier to get to that point by knowing how to remember individual words and make *them* part of you first. This is where this chapter comes into play; by following the techniques involved, the retention of new words will be easy, and fun.

First of all, please realize that, in a sense, learning how to remember foreign words will be very similar to how we learned English words in the previous chapter. Since you didn't know their meanings (assuming you didn't), weren't they *foreign* to you? The only difference in this case is that, depending on the particular language, word pronunciations will often be a bit different from what we would assume them to be in English. Two points right here: First, if you were studying a foreign language, the first thing you would learn is how to pronounce the various letters. Second, you would learn the exact pronunciation of each individual word. Therefore, as long as I get close to the correct pronunciation, with a little bit of imagination on your part, the Soundalikes we use will make sense.

First let's learn some Spanish words.

Mesa, pronounced "`may sa," means *table* . The Soundalike I use for mesa is "mess." Now that we can picture *mesa,* via the Soundalike *mess,* let's associate that with its English counterpart, table. In your mind's eye, picture a table in your home being a real mess. That's all there is to it! Let's do one more in detail:

Seguro, pronounced "sa `gore o," is equivalent to the English word *insurance*. A good Soundalike for *seguro* is the word, "secure." Now, to associate the word *secure* with *insurance* is easy isn't it? Just imagine feeling very secure because you have taken out a new insurance policy.

Let's now go through some more Spanish words in the same way that we learned English words in the previous chapter. The only difference in the setup will be that the pronunciation of each word will be given immediately following the foreign word. Again, have fun with these, and every so often give yourself a review of the words you just learned. In no time, you will *own* them.

Botones "bow `tone ays" (buttons)—*bellboy*. Picture the bellboy's uniform having thousands of buttons on it.

Boleto "bow `let o" (bullet)—*ticket*. See yourself shooting a gun at a ticket. The bullet goes right through it.

Pregunta "pray `goon ta" (pregnant)—*question*. Imagine a pregnant woman asking a lot of questions.

Recado "rek `a doe" (record)—*message*. Did you record the message?

Arroz "a `roze" (arrows)—*rice*. See yourself shooting arrows at a bowl of rice, or maybe picture the pieces of rice as tiny arrows.

Commenzar "comb men `zar" (commence)—*to begin*. If you know that commence means begin, then that is all the clue you need.

Rey "ray" (Ray)—*king*. Imagine someone you know named Ray, being a king.

Mayor "my `or" (mayor)—*older*. Picture your city's mayor being older than you are.

Cinturon "sin too `ron" (sin you ran)—*belt*. It's a sin you ran without wearing your belt. That's why your pants fell down.

Impuesto "im `pwest o" (pest)—*tax*. Don't you agree that having to pay tax can be a real pest?

Abrigo "a `bree go" (a bridge)—*overcoat*. See yourself wearing a bridge as an overcoat. Or putting thousands of overcoats over a bridge.

Ropa "`rope a" (rope)—*clothing*. Picture yourself wearing ropes instead of conventional clothing.

Negocio "nay `go see o" (negotiate)—*business*. Having to negotiate is an important part of business, isn't it?

Boda "`bow da" (boat)—*wedding*. Picture your friend's wedding taking place on a boat.

Mantequilla "mahn tay `key ya" (Monty kill ya')—*butter*. My buddy Monty will kill ya' if you take the butter.

Pan "pahn" (pan)—*bread*. See yourself trying to fry a gigantic loaf of bread in a tiny frying pan.

Sopa "`so pa" (soap)—*soup*. That bowl of soup tastes terrible. Imagine the taste of soup with soap in it. Yeeech! At least it will remind me not to use dirty words.

Frito "`free toes" (Frito's)—*fried*. Frito's Corn Chips™ are basically fried corn chips.

Revuelto "rev `welt o" (revolve)—*scrambled*. If you keep revolving an egg, it will eventually become scrambled.

Cuchara "coo `cha ra" (cute Charo)—*spoon*. Remember cute Charo, the guitarist from Spain? Picture her playing her guitar with a spoon.

Horno "horn o" (horn)—*oven*. Imagine there is a gigantic horn cooking in your oven. When you open the oven door to take it out, you are surprised when the horn sounds very loudly.

Cansado "cahn `sahd o" (can sad)—*tired*. Picture a tin can being very sad because it is so tired.

Avion "ah vee `own" (aviation)—*airplane*. This one speaks for itself, doesn't it?

Dientes "dee `en taze" (dentist)—*teeth*. Wow! Another one that fits right in.

Pajaro "pa `ha row" (park car o)—*bird*. Imagine a bird driving a car. Now he parks the car on a gigantic Cheerio™.

Preocupar "pray ok you `pahr" (preoccupied)—*to worry*. Again, it works out naturally.

Florecer "floor ay `sayr" (floral)—*to bloom*. Notice how the floral arrangement really blooms.

Now let's try our hand with some French words:

Visage "vee `zahj" (massage)—*face*. Picture yourself getting a facial massage.

Songer "son `jay" (sun)—*dream*. Imagine yourself having a dream about the sun.

Beaucoup "bow `coo" (bow cute)—*a lot, much*. See lots and lots of bows. Aren't they all cute?

Cicatrice "sick a `tris" (sick trees)—*scar*. Picture a bunch of sick trees as having deep scars.

Parlez-vous Français?

Champignon "shom pig `nyon" (champagne)—*mushroom*. See a bunch of mushrooms drinking champagne.

Toujours "too `jur" (told ya')—*always*. It's always the same. I told ya' and told ya' but you wouldn't listen.

Avocat "ah voe `ka" (avocado)—*lawyer*. Imagine an avocado being a lawyer, presenting its case in court.

Choux "shoe" (shoe)—*cabbages*. Picture a bunch of cabbages wearing gigantic shoes. Or, see yourself wearing cabbages on your feet instead of shoes.

Ecole "`eh cole" (he call)—*school*. He calls us when it's time for school.

Bibliothèque "bibliotek" (bibles talk)—*library*. Only bibles are allowed to talk in the library.

Pont "pohn" (punt)—*bridge*. See yourself punting a football over the bridge.

Cheveux "sha va" (shiver)—*hair*. Picture your hair being so cold it begins to shiver.

Plage "plahj"—*plush*. It all sounds alike, doesn't it?

Coussin "coo sehn" (cousin)—*pillow*. Imagine having a pillow for a cousin.

Maison "may `zon" (mason)—*House*. Picture a brick mason building your house.

Enfant "ahn `fahn" (infant)—*child*. Works right in, doesn't it?

Let's look at some words in Italian now.

Piccolo "`pick o low" (piccolo)—*small*. See a person playing a piccolo. It's a small piccolo, however, so you can hardly see it.

Primavera "pree ma `vehr a" (prime fair)—*spring*. The spring is an excellent (prime) time to have the fair come to town.

> **Do you speak Italian?**

77

Gamba "`gahm ba" (gamble)—*leg*. Imagine a person gambling away his leg in a poker game.

Fumo "`foo moe" (fume)—*smoke*. Another easy one.

Pericoloso "perry coe `low so" (Perry colossal)—*dangerous*. Picture a person named Perry being so colossal that he is dangerous.

Dolce "`dole chay" (Dole)—*sweet*. See yourself biting into a Dole™ pineapple. It is very sweet.

Mangiare "mahn `jar ay" (munch jar)—*to eat*. You want to eat so you munch on a jar. Yeech!

Lacrima "`la cree ma" (cream)—*tear*. Imagine that you are crying. Instead of a tear, cream comes out of your eyes.

Stanco "`stahn koe" (stand)—*tired*. You are tired from standing for so long.

Frate "`frah tay" (fraternity)—*brother*. Speaks for itself, right?

My friend Renata is originally from Yugoslavia, and she was kind enough to share with us some words from her native language, which is Serbo-Croatian.

Bazen "`bah zhen" (bathing)—*pool*. See yourself bathing in your pool.

Lopta "`lowp ta" (lobbed the)—*ball*. Instead of throwing it hard, you lobbed the ball.

Plaza "`plah zhah" (pleasure)—*beach*. On a hot day, it can be a real pleasure to go to the beach.

Brkovi "brah `coe vee" (break off me)—*mustache*. My mustache was so hard, it could break right off me.

Sutra "`suit ra" (suit)—*tomorrow*. Remember to wear your suit tomorrow.

Jabuka "ya `book ah" (your book)—*apple*. Picture yourself taking your book and eating it like an apple.

Serbo-Croatian?

Sladoled "`sluhd oh led" (sled of lead)—*ice cream*. Picture a gallon of ice cream riding on the back of a sled that is made of lead.

Hvala "h `va la" (koala)—*thank you*. See a koala bear thanking you for something. Maybe for not flying Quantis.

Ne brini "nay `breeny" (neigh, bring me)—*don't worry*. See a horse (Mr. Ed?) saying to you, "Neigh, bring me another carrot, and don't worry, carrots are very healthy."

Dovidenja "dove ee `jayn ya" (dove of ginger)—*goodbye*. Picture a gingerbread dove (dove of ginger), telling you "goodbye".

Prst "perst" (pressed)—*finger*. You pressed your finger on something so hard that it hurt.

Petak "pet `ahk" (pay check)—*Friday*. Alas, it makes sense all by itself once again.

Yes, from Spanish to Serbo-Croatian, and everything or anything in between, this system will enable you to more easily and effectively learn new words in any language. Just use the techniques you know, including a heavy dose of imagination, and you will be able to do it. Look over the words you just learned and quiz yourself whenever you like. After a short time you will know them without needing the mnemonics involved.

What I would really suggest, however, is that you concentrate on learning as many words as you can in the language you are currently studying. If you haven't taken up another language, what's keeping you? Courses abound in most areas. I belong to a small group that meets at our teacher's home once a week, and it's great fun. Go for it. You'll breeze through the vocabulary.

Remember Numbers Via The Mnemonic Alphabet

> *"Every great discovery I ever made, I gambled that the truth was there, and then I acted on it in faith until I could prove its existence."*
> *Arthur H. Compton*
> *(Nobel-winning physicist)*

The concepts and techniques you'll learn in this chapter will truly pioneer your lift to "memory greatness." Primarily, the information will show you a nifty way to master the ability to remember numbers. Then, combined with the next chapter, it will help you remember all kinds of information. **Warning:** At first, the explanation will seem confusing, if not downright strange. Of course, you are already used to that.

Please Don't Be Intimidated

For the next several pages you may find it difficult to understand why you are doing the exercises I am having you do. As I've said before, and will continue to say throughout this book, don't worry. By the time you finish this chapter, you will understand its significance and incredible application in working with and remembering numbers of all kinds.

Aren't numbers difficult? I know that a certain percentage of the population such as accountants, math teachers and others who were blessed with a natural ability to work with numbers will answer, "No Bob, they're not." I'm sure that is the case for them. But for most of us, numbers, along with people's names, have to be about the most difficult thing to remember. And why is that? Simply because numbers are intangible. They are nothing more than geometrical shapes and designs with absolutely no rhyme or reason. In other words, what makes *7* a seven? What makes *3* a three? What gives *5382* the value of five thousand, three hundred eighty-two? Think about it for a moment.

Remember that list you linked together earlier, beginning with thumbtacks and ending with map? Once you learned how to link two items together, one you already knew with one you wanted to remember, it was merely a matter of taking an item that you pictured in your mind's eye and associating it with another image you pictured. Fine. But then in the next exercise, it was a bit more difficult because you had to associate items, or names in this case, that were intangible, or difficult to picture.

However, after you learned about the Soundalike, which takes the intangible and turns it into something you can see or picture, the process was a whole lot easier, wasn't it? Now, what is even more difficult is picturing numbers in a way that you can see them. Good news: numbers, even sequences of numbers come alive like color cartoons once you liberate them from their closet of intangibility.

We Must Be Able To Picture Them

For example, phone numbers, addresses, serial numbers, account numbers and many other numbers tend to be difficult for most people to remember, because unless something can be pictured, it is less likely to be remembered.

One might be tempted to argue with that last statement, but really, isn't it true? Think of anything and you come up with a picture. Just like when I say to you, "Whatever you do, please don't think of a purple elephant." What picture flashes through your mind? Of course, a purple elephant. At least an elephant, if not a purple one. And those who tend to be naturally fantastic with numbers tell me that they somehow seem to be able to picture numbers in a way that makes them make sense.

If you are thinking, "Well, I *can* picture numbers," I would respond: sure, we all can to a certain point, but just try to remember a phone number after listening to the 411 computer voice. You dial the number without writing it down and the line is busy. Have you ever had to waste your time and money redialing Directory Assistance because you had already forgotten the number? Many people have, because they have not been able to lock into their minds a picture of what those numbers represent.

Here's How We Do It

Down to cases, then. There are only ten Arabic numbers. They are: one, two, three, four, five, six, seven, eight, nine, and zero. That is it! Any other numbers, through infinity, are merely combinations of those ten. And luckily enough, do you realize that, for all intents and purposes, there are also only ten basic consonant sounds in the English language? That's right, only ten basic consonant sounds. "Well Bob," you may be wondering, "there are 21 consonants. How could there be only ten consonant sounds?"

If you have ever taken a speech pathology class, or studied phonics, you were shown how to shape and form your mouth in order to pronounce the various letters and sounds. Certain consonant sounds which we know as being different are actually shaped and formed in the same way.

For instance, take the letters *T* and *D*. Out loud, please say the letter, *T*. Notice where your tongue hits your teeth and the roof of your mouth. Observe the same thing as you say the letter *D*. Incredible, isn't it? I want you to forget about the slight difference in these two sounds, because for the most part, they are the same. And you will be able to take advantage of these similarities for the rest of your life, once you learn how it is done.

Now, out loud, please make the sounds created by pronouncing the letters *J, CH*, soft *G*, and *SH*. Notice the very same thing?

Fine. Now pronounce out loud the sounds for the letters hard *C, K* and hard *G*. Great! See what I mean? They each have the guttural sound that is formed in the back of the throat.

Now try it for the letters *F, V* and *PH*. Aren't they, as are the other groups, pronounced the same as far as your ears, but especially teeth, tongue, and even lips, are concerned? Absolutely. The same goes for the letters *P* and *B*. That is known as the "explosion of air" sound. Put your hand in front of your mouth as you pronounce either of those letters and you will understand why. Now, just one more grouping. Please make the sounds caused by pronouncing the letters *Z*, soft *C* and *S*. Worked again, right? We've just duplicated six consonant sounds. With the four remaining, that brings us to an even ten, doesn't it?

The four other consonant sounds are those we hear when pronouncing the letters, *N*-nuh, *M*-muh, *R*-ruh and *L*-luh. At this time, we are going to assign each of these ten sounds a number value. Notice what is happening. There are ten basic Arabic numbers and ten basic consonant sounds. We are going to match them up. And again, I realize that at this point in time you have no idea where this is leading. Please be patient. We will get to that real soon.

For now, please accept the fact that number one is always represented by the sound caused by pronouncing the letters *T* and *D*. **Very important point right here:** You do *not* have to remember that the number one is represented by the *letters T* and *D* because we are not interested in the letters, only the sounds. Keep in mind that we have established, for the sake of this system, that the sounds made by pronouncing the letters *T* and *D* are the same. Here is an easy way of remembering that the number one is represented by the "tuh" and "duh" sound. There is one downstroke in the letter *T*. That will help you to associate the *1* and the *T*. When you remember that, your natural memory will tell you that the number 1 is also represented by the sound made by pronouncing the letter *D*.

Easy Ways To Remember The Rest

The number 2 is represented by the sound made when pronouncing the letter *N*, or nuh. You can remember this by noticing that there are two downstrokes in the written letter N.

The number 3 is represented by the "muh" sound, made by pronouncing the letter *M*. You can remember that by noticing that there are three downstrokes in the letter *M*.

Next is the number 4. That is represented by the "ruh" sound of the letter R. How do you remember that? There are four letters in the number four, the last letter being **RRRR**.

The number *5* is represented by the "luh" sound of *L*. To remember this, hold up your left hand, palm away, with the four fingers together and the thumb outstretched. What letter do you see? That's right, the L.

The next number, 6, is represented by the sound made when pronouncing the letters J, CH, soft G, SH, DG and TCH. This can easily be remembered by noticing that the number 6 and the letter J are mirror images of each other. Please remember not to worry about learning letters, only the sounds. You do not have to remember that 6 is represented by the letters J, CH, soft G, SH, DG and TCH, only by the common sound made by all six.

The number 7 is represented by the sounds of hard C, K, and hard G. Here is the way to remember that. If you take two sevens and butt-end them together, you will form an abstract K. You may need to really use the ol' imagination for that one. However, because of that, it will probably be the easiest to remember.

The number 8 is represented by the sounds made by the letters F, V and PH. This can easily be remembered by noticing that the number 8 has two loops. How many loops does the written f have? And of course you now know that if you correlate the number 8 to the "fuh" sound of the letter F, then that is what is important. The other two letters have the same sound, don't they? You could also play off the letter V and the number 8 by picturing V-8 Juice™.

1	T,D, TH* — The letter T has *one* downstroke.	
2	N — The written letter n has *two* downstrokes.	
3	M —The letter M has *three* downstrokes.	
4	R — The word *four* is spelled *f-o-u-RRRRRRR*.	
5	L — Hold up your left hand, palm away from you, with the four fingers together and the thumb outstretched. The four fingers and thumb form an L.	
6	J, CH, soft G, SH, DG, TCH — The number 6 and the letter *J* are mirror images.	
7	K, hard C, hard G, Q — Two "7s" butted together form a K.	
8.	F, V, PH — The number 8 and the written f each contain two loops. Or what about V-8 Juice™?	
9	P, B — The number 9 and the letter P are mirror images.	
0	Z, soft C, S — The word *zero* begins with a Z.	

*Why does the sound made by pronouncing the letters TH have the value of 1, the same as T and D? Because the sound made by forming and pronouncing the letters TH is basically an American sound. Anyone who attempts to learn the English language after his/her patterns of speech have already been formed has a very difficult time pronouncing the "TH" sound. For instance, when trying to say the phrase, "the thing," it will come out as "da ting." I've heard this over and over again during classes I have taught. And those of a foreign language origin always make a point of agreeing with me on this.

The number *9* is represented by the "puh" and "buh" sounds made by pronouncing the letters *P* and *B*. The way to remember that *9* is represented by that sound is by noticing that the number *9* and the letter *P* are mirror images of each other. In fact, if you want, you can even turn the *P* upside down and you will have a *b*.

And finally, the number *0*, which is represented by the sounds made by pronouncing the letters *Z*, soft *C* and *S*. This one is probably the easiest to remember because zero sounds just like the sounds made by pronouncing those letters.

Note: The vowels *A, E, I, O, U* have absolutely no numerical value in this system. Neither do the letters *W, H, Y*. (WHY?) The only exception is the letter H, which at times will immediately follow a consonant, thereby changing that consonant's sound. Example: "TH," "CH," "SH," and "PH."

The Sounds Are The Key

IMPORTANT!... IMPORTANT!... IMPORTANT! We are interested only in sounds, not letters. Using the memory aids I have given you, take some time and commit the Mnemonic Alphabet to memory. You can practice by putting a piece of paper over the numbers column and deciding what the correct sounds (not letters) are. You could also try covering the sounds column and figuring out the correct numbers. Switching back and forth quicker and quicker will also help.

Another good idea is to have a friend, spouse or family member take turns calling out the different numbers, while you respond with the correct sounds. Then have your helper call out the different sounds and you answer with the correct numbers.

Flash cards are also helpful. You will see your response times reduced to conditioned reflexes. Review several times for about fifteen minutes each time, and I'm telling you, you will know the Mnemonic Alphabet frontwards and backwards. And you need to in order to master this system. I realize you still don't know why you are doing this, so I will ask you to just go along with me for now. The fun will begin real, real soon. After you have learned the Mnemonic Alphabet, please go on to the next exercise.

A Worthwhile Exercise

Please make yourself invest a few more moments to do this next drill. The exercise will accomplish two things. First, it will reinforce what you have learned, while putting the Mnemonic Alphabet to memory. Second, it will emphasize the importance of sounds as opposed to letters. Notice that in the first column of words I have underlined the sounds. All you need to do is figure out their number values, like the examples *book, cat*, and, even *encyclopedia*. The next two columns are left up to you. First, figure out the consonant sounds that receive numerical value, then decide on that value. As you will see, I went through the list and filled some of them in for you. Explanations about those words follow the exercise. Until one is used to the Mnemonic Alphabet, it can sometimes be just a bit tricky. And I am definitely not trying to trick you. I simply want to make it easier for you to learn than it was for me.

What Are The Values For These Words?
(Concentrate on sounds, not letters.)

book _____ 97	file _____	nobody _____
cat _____ 71	world _____	projector _____
radio _____	nieces _____	furniture _____ 84264
telephone _____	folder _____	record _____
desk _____	teacher _____	hydrogen _____
news _____	print _____	ox _____ 70
nose _____	train _____	excellence _____ 70520
paper _____	bicycle _____	candle _____
tam _____	spinach _____	picture _____ 9764
chum _____	post _____	celebrate _____
system _____	morning _____	cleansers _____
trophy _____	thread _____	dictionary _____ 17624
stars _____	dance _____	towel _____
lunar _____	factory _____	bibliography _____
pamphlet _____	toad _____	athletics _____
briefcase _____	percent _____	switches _____ 060
chair _____	speak _____	condition _____
basket _____	machine _____	travel _____
portrait _____	chief _____	education _____ 6762
encyclopedia _____ 207591	chef _____	graphic _____
apple _____	senate _____	unlimited _____
America _____	rain _____	periodical _____
wood _____	daylight _____	positive _____
arm _____	sneakers _____	champion _____
town _____	player _____	ball _____

Correct values are on page 91.

87

Here are some comments for words/numerical values that may have seemed somewhat complicated:

encyclopedia — 207591
Notice that one *C* is representative of the number *0* and the very next *C* representative of the number *7*

furniture — 84264
The *T* in this case is actually representative of the number *6*

ox — 70
Note that the letter *X* has the sound of hard *C* and *S*

excellence — 70520
You only hear the first *L*

picture — 9764
Again, the letter *T* is representative of the number *6*

dictionary — 17624
That darn *T* again! It takes on the value of *S* or *6*

switches — 060
All three letters account for one sound, right?

education — 6762
This one may take some thought. It does for me every time I look at it!

Good For You

Congratulations for having the tenacity to complete these drills. First, by committing the Mnemonic Alphabet to memory, and then by filling in those word values. So now you're asking, "Well, Burg, I did as you asked. Now explain what good it's going to do me." At this point, I can only give you a hint: Knowing the Mnemonic Alphabet and understanding the previously learned Chain Link Method and Soundalike, combined with the mental, or mind, hooks you will learn in the next chapter, will allow you to commit any number to memory.

All Right, If You Insist

So you don't want to wait until after the next chapter. Fine. Let's do this then. How about if I give you some quick examples to show you how what you learned in this chapter will help you master remembering those intangible numbers? We'll begin with a social security number. Let's use 029-45-3214. Incidentally, I just grabbed those numbers out of thin air. I hope they don't really belong to anybody. I know some people who have had their social security number for 20 years and still don't know it. We are going to learn this one in no time.

Take the numbers *029*. Using the Mnemonic Alphabet, transpose them into a word or words that give you a picture, something you can see. How about s_un u_p? Can you see why the words *sun up* must equal *029*?

Now a word picture for *45*. One of several words that would work is ra_il, as in railroad tracks.

Finally, the last four digits, *3214*. One word picture that certainly fits is me_ntor, which is another word for personal teacher. So we have the words *sun up, rail* and *mentor.*

Let's Bring It Together

Now we are going to have our ol' buddy the Chain Link Method step in and help us commit that to memory. First, take the item in question, the social security card, and make it gigantic in your mind's eye. Now, stick it as hard as you can into the sun as it begins its rise up into the sky. At this point, during sun up, you can see the social security card shining brightly. And because you associated that card with s_un u_p, you know its first three numbers have to be 029.

The next word picture is "rail." In your mind's eye, see a gigantic rail forming across the sky. See that sun riding along the rail at a great rate of speed, trying as hard as it can not to fall off. If you remember ra_il, you know the next two numbers of the card are 45.

Finally, in order to remember the last four numbers, picture in your mind's eye the person you consider to be your <u>mentor</u>. See him/her frowning disapprovingly over what is taking place.

Now go over that sequence of pictures several times. About an hour from now, do it again. And if you will review it one more time tomorrow, you will probably be able to remember that number for as long as you want. Naturally, in this case, assuming that 029-45-3214 is not your social security number, you have absolutely no need to remember it. Because of that, you probably won't. I certainly wouldn't. But it does make good practice.

How About Another?

Next, let's put your checking account number to memory. Let's say the number happens to be 14970003479. Child's play. First, break up the numbers into four groups. 149-<u>trip</u>, 700-<u>cusses</u>, 034-<u>summer</u>, 79-<u>cup</u>. There are, of course, several different word pictures you could have come up with for each of these number combinations. Those are just the ones I happened to see.

You know what to do from here, don't you? In your mind's eye, take the object you wish to remember, your checking account number, and simply picture your checkbook. As you are running with your checkbook in hand, you suddenly <u>trip</u> (149) and fall down flat. You're angry, and <u>cusses</u> (700) are coming out of your mouth with wild abandon—naughty, naughty! But you soon realize you shouldn't be mad because at least the <u>summer</u> (034) weather is beautiful. In fact, you decide to cool off with a deliciously cold <u>cup</u> (79) of lemonade. Again, go over that Chain Link story in your mind's eye several times and it will be yours for as long as you wish to keep it.

Do They All Fit?

What happens if you can't think of word pictures for certain numbers? Well, it's definitely true that for certain numbers that are three digits or longer, you and I, together, would be hard pressed to come up with a word picture. However, you can always come up with a word picture for two-digit numbers, and then link with a word picture for the remaining digit. In the next chapter, we will learn those one- and two-digit word pictures.

St. Francis of Assisi was hoeing his garden when someone asked him what he would do if he were suddenly to learn that he would die before sunset that very day. "I would finish hoeing my garden," he replied.

This process, by the way, can be used for any long-digit number. And it doesn't matter how long that number is because you can link together as many word pictures as you like. Of course, the longer the number, the more time it will take to put to memory. But imagine how long it would take to put 029-45-3214 or 14970003479 to memory without the use of this system.

What Are The Values For These Words?
(Answers to exercise on page 87.)

book 97	file 85	nobody 291
cat 71	world 451	projector 946714
radio 41	nieces 200	furniture 84264
telephone 1582	folder 8514	record 4741
desk 107	teacher 164	hydrogen 1462
news 20	print 941	ox 70
nose 20	train 142	excellence 70520
paper 994	bicycle 9075	candle 7215
tam 13	spinach 0926	picture 9764
chum 63	post 901	celebrate 05941
system 0013	morning 34227	cleansers 752040
trophy 148	thread 141	dictionary 17624
stars 0140	dance 120	towel 15
lunar 524	factory 8714	bibliography 995748
pamphlet 93851	toad 11	athletics 15170
briefcase 94870	percent 94021	switches 060
chair 64	speak 097	condition 72162
basket 9071	machine 362	travel 1485
portrait 94141	chief 68	education 6762
encyclopedia 207591	chef 68	graphic 7487
apple 95	senate 021	unlimited 25311
America 347	rain 42	periodical 94175
wood 1	daylight 151	positive 9018
arm 43	sneakers 02740	champion 6392
town 12	player 954	ball 95

Mental Hooks

What Would It Be Worth To You?

How many times have we all wished that we had available to us an emergency memory pill that we could take any time we forgot something of significance? If you are like I was, then probably quite often. In fact, I will often ask my audience, "How much money would you give me if I could supply you with pills that would allow you to significantly increase your ability to remember anything? You wouldn't have to take the time or make the effort to study any of the techniques we are currently learning. You would only have to take a pill whenever necessary." Responses are hilarious, as they reach into six figures and sometimes more. It's true. It would be an incredible seller. Unfortunately, a memory-loss panacea has not yet been discovered, and I doubt it ever will be. Until such time as it is on the market and affordable, learning our techniques is really the best way, and fun as well.

Also, as suggestions of memory remedies, cures and elixirs have come and gone, these techniques have proven themselves. The reason I make this point as we head into Chapter 8 is that this is the last time I will ask you to study and learn material before knowing exactly how you will put it to work in everyday life. So just bear with me a bit longer.

First, please note once again the Mnemonic Alphabet and the words directly across.

Mnemonic Alphabet Values	Mental Hooks
1. T,D, TH	1. <u>T</u>oe
2. Noah	2. <u>N</u>oah
3. Ma	3. <u>M</u>a
4. Row	4. <u>R</u>ow
5. Law	5. <u>L</u>aw
6. J, CH, soft G, SH, DG, TCH	6. <u>Ch</u>ow
7. K, hard C, hard G, Q	7. <u>C</u>ow
8. F, V, PH	8. <u>F</u>oe
9. P, B	9. <u>B</u>oy
10. Z, soft C, S	10. <u>T</u>ie<u>s</u>

Let's examine these ten, and first understand what we are doing. Again, I realize that for now you don't know why, but I promise, you will. Do you see how we come up with the word *Toe* for number 1, and why the letter *T* is underlined? The reason is that the *T* in Toe, the "tuh" sound, has the value of *1* in our Mnemonic Alphabet, and of course the *o* and *e,* being vowels, don't count, do they? Before going on, please make sure you understand that concept. Now, assuming you do, I am going to ask you to picture, in your *mind's eye,* your big toe. Once you understand the purpose, and see the results it will bring, then for the rest of your life that mental picture of your big toe will always be representative of the number *1.*

The Mental Hook for number 2 is *Noah*, with the letter *N* underlined. And why is that? Correct—the "nuh" sound of *N* is equal to the number 2, and the other letters, being vowels and an *h*, do not have any numerical value in this system. For Noah, I suggest picturing an old man with a gray beard on an ark. Again, for the rest of your life, the mental picture of Noah will always be representative of the number 2.

For number 3 we have *Ma*, slang for mother. The *M* is underlined and the vowel *a* doesn't count. Simply picture your ma in your mind's eye.

For number 4 we have the word *Row*. The letter *R* is underlined. The *o*, being a vowel, is not and of course the *w* isn't either. For row, let's picture a long row in a garden.

Next to number 5 in our list of mental hooks you can see the word *Law*. By now you should know why the letter *L* is underlined, and the *a* and *w* are not. The "luh" sound of the letter *L* has the numerical value of 5, while the *a* and the *w* have no numerical value, because *a* is a vowel and *w* is one of the other three letters in our Mnemonic Alphabet that also have no numerical value. For the word *law*, let's picture in our mind's eye a police officer. This police officer can be either a man or woman, your favorite law officer, or the one who just gave you a speeding ticket for travelling 46 mph in a 45 mph zone. It doesn't matter whom you picture; however, you must always picture that same law officer every time you need to picture the word *law* for number 5.

Mental hook number 6 is the word *Chow*. Notice which letters are underlined. The *C* and *H*. And do you know why? That's right, because the "chuh" sound of the letters *CH* has the numerical value of *6* in our Mnemonic alphabet. Of course the *o* and the *e,* being vowels, do not count. If you are wondering why the *H* counts, please keep in mind that even though the *H* does not usually have any numerical value in the system, it does when following another consonant, changing that consonant's sound, as it does in this case. For *chow*, I suggest picturing a giant cereal bowl.

Moving right along to number 7, you can see that the Mental Hook is *Cow*. The *C* is underlined, the *o* and the *w* are not. When I first began teaching the system, I was living in Oklahoma, and I used to tell the students to simply picture *their* cow, because practically everyone in Oklahoma owned a cow. (I say that tongue-in-cheek, of course; not everyone owned a cow. I knew one person who didn't.) Since most of us don't own a cow, however, I will suggest instead that you picture any cow, a generic cow, or even Elsie the cow. It doesn't really matter, so long as you always picture that same cow every time for number 7.

For Mental Hook number 8 we have the word *Foe*, which is an

enemy. In this case, your personal enemy. You know why the *F* is underlined and the other two letters are not, so the only thing you need to do now is get a picture in your mind's eye of your worst foe. If you are one of those people lucky enough not to have a foe, then fine, make one up. And remember to always use that same foe every time for number 8.

Next to number 9 is the word *Boy*. The *B* is underlined; the *o* and the *y* are not. Picture either your little boy, or your nephew, or some other little boy who means something special to you. For instance, in my case, two of my best friends had a little-five-year old boy by the name of Mark. Mark was the little boy I pictured then, and even though I haven't seen him for several years and he probably looks different from when I knew him, I still use that same picture of the five-year-old boy, Mark. And 50 years from now I still will, because the pictures we use for the individual Mental Hooks never change.

And finally, to round out the first ten of the 20 upon which we will concentrate, we have the word *Ties*. You will notice that the letters *t* and *s* are underlined, and the letters *i* and *e* are not. Let's do this explanation backwards. The *i* and the *e* are vowels, thus they have no numerical value. You know that, so what about the letters *t* and *s*? Note that the tuh sound, or the letter *t*, corresponds with the number *1* of our Mnemonic Alphabet. That's where we get the first digit in the number *10*. Meanwhile, the "suh" sound, or the letter *s*, corresponds with the number *0* of our Mnemonic Alphabet. That's where we get the second digit. Put the *1* and the *0* together and what do you get? Yes, the number *10*. And for the number *10*, you should always picture several of your favorite or least favorite ties.

Why These Particular Pictures?

All right, the first ten completed, we have ten more to go and I'll share with you the magic of the hooks. First, a couple of quick points. Please notice the common traits of our first ten Mental Hooks. Number one, they are all tangible items. You can picture them. In the last chapter, we learned that it is much easier to remember numbers when you can see them, didn't we? And number two, they are all distinct, separate from one another. There is no confusing any of those pictures with the others, is there? Those two traits will continue throughout the Mental Hooks we will learn. By the way, you may have asked, "Why should we necessarily use these particular word pictures for our Mental Hooks when many other possibilities spring to mind as well?"

For instance, hook number 1 could have been *tie, tee, tea, to, two, too* or *toy* to name just a few. Mental Hook number 2 could have been *knee, neigh, new, knew, gnu, no* or *know,* as well as some others. And how about hook number 10? *Toes, tees, teas, tease, dice, days, daze, doze,* and again, probably many more would have fit according to our Mnemonic Alphabet. The key is to keep them all tangible and distinct, undeniably separate from each other. If we had used *tie* for number 1 and *ties* for number 10, that would have been confusing, right? And you will soon see why they must sparkle with their own personality, so to speak. Let's move on by completing our list of Mental Hooks through number 20.

Mnemonic Alphabet Values	Mental Hooks	Mental Hooks
1. T, D, TH 1	1. Toe	11. Toad
2. N	2. Noah	12. Tin
3. M	3. Ma	13. Tam
4. R	4. Row	14. Tree
5. L	5. Law	15. Towel
6. J,CH, soft G, SH,DG,TCH	6. Chow	16. Teach
7. K, hard C, CK, hard G, Q	7. Cow	17. Tack
8. F, V, PH	8. Foe	18. Taffy
9. P, B	9. Boy	19. Tub
10. Z, soft C, S	10. Ties	20. Nose

For hooks 11 through 19 we know that the first consonant sound must either be the "tuh," "nuh," or "thu" sound, don't we? (We'll explain number 20 when we come to it.) And that the last consonant sound will correspond with its number in the Mnemonic Alphabet. For example, Mental Hook number 11 is *Toad,* for which we would

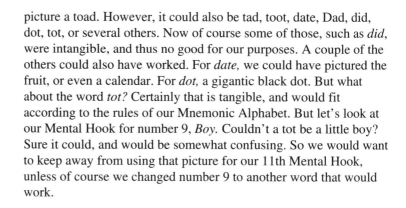

picture a toad. However, it could also be tad, toot, date, Dad, did, dot, tot, or several others. Now of course some of those, such as *did*, were intangible, and thus no good for our purposes. A couple of the others could also have worked. For *date,* we could have pictured the fruit, or even a calendar. For *dot,* a gigantic black dot. But what about the word *tot?* Certainly that is tangible, and would fit according to the rules of our Mnemonic Alphabet. But let's look at our Mental Hook for number 9, *Boy.* Couldn't a tot be a little boy? Sure it could, and would be somewhat confusing. So we would want to keep away from using that picture for our 11th Mental Hook, unless of course we changed number 9 to another word that would work.

What I am going to ask you to do however, for right now anyway, is to humor me with the Mental Hooks I am providing. They have been tested for usability, and until you become experienced enough with this system to understand why some words would work as Mental Hooks better than others, and make them up yourself, I would suggest you stick with these. Now let's quickly move on.

The Mental Hook for number 12 is *Tin.* Picture tin foil, or Reynolds Wrap™, or anything else tin brings to mind for you. Maybe the Tin Man from the Wizard of Oz. Incidentally, I will no longer bother pointing out the letters that are and are not underlined. At this point I am sure you know the rules.

The Mental Hook for number 13 is *Tam,* which is a type of hat originating from Scotland. It looks somewhat like a derby, so just picture that in your mind's eye. I always picture a gigantic, bright orange tam.

Mental Hook number 14 is *Tree.* If you had a favorite tree that you climbed or enjoyed as a child, fine. If not, then simply come up with a mental picture of any tree you would like.

Mental Hook number 15 is *Towel.* A mental picture of any towel will do fine here. Keep in mind though, the more outlandish you make your garish, technicolor hunk of terry cloth, the more effective it will be.

The Mental Hook for number 16 is *Teach*. I know, the word teach is a verb, and not tangible. Well, let's use our imagination and make it tangible by picturing either our favorite or least favorite teacher from school days.

Mental Hook number 17 is *Tag*. For tag, I suggest picturing a gigantic price tag you might find on an item at the department store.

The Mental Hook for number 18 is *Taffy*. (Remember, we only pronounce and/or hear the first *f* ; that's why it isn't 188.) For this, a mental picture of gigantic pieces of taffy, or a long piece of taffy being made will work out just fine.

Mental Hook number 19 is *Tub*. Simply picture your bathtub.

Now for Mental Hook number 20. You will notice from your chart the twentieth Mental Hook happens to be *Nose*. If you already know why nose would work for number 20, that's great. Otherwise, please follow along and I believe you will have it momentarily. The first consonant sound, in order to match the first number in 20, which is 2, must have the "nuh" sound of 2 in our Mnemonic Alphabet. The second consonant sound, in order to match the second number in 20, which is 0, must have the "zuh" or "suh" sound of zero in our Mnemonic Alphabet. There are, of course, several other words that conceivably could work. Knees and niece to name two. But we are going to use "nose." Picturing your very own nose will work best.

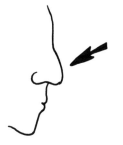

A Quick Review

Take a few minutes to review your Mental Hooks. At this point, you don't have to commit them to memory; however, eventually you must if you are to master this system. Not to worry. It isn't particularly difficult, and you don't even have to know them flawlessly. What's nice is that the more you use them, the more adept you will become; until one day soon you will discover you know your Mental Hooks flawlessly. After the upcoming mind-blowing exercise, I will show you an easy way to commit the Mental Hooks to memory. Now, please take just a few minutes to review your Mental Hooks, and then read on.

The Mental Hooks have many uses. Remembering lists of items in and out of sequence is a good one with which to begin. Do you recall the first time we used the Chain Link Method to remember a list of ten items? We remembered those items both frontwards and backwards, but if I asked you which item was sixth on that list, you would have had to stop and think about it, wouldn't you? In fact, you would have had to start with the first item and work your way up, or begin with the last item and work your way down. That isn't the case with your Mental Hooks. And why not? It is again based on the principle that memory is the association of two items: one you already know with another you wish to remember. Once you have your Mental Hooks committed to memory, they will always be what you already know, and you will merely associate that hook with the item you wish to remember. Let's work with a couple of examples.

In a previous list, the sixth item was *magazine.* Associating the number *6* with magazine might be a bit difficult, because the number *6* is merely a geometrical design, and, as we discussed earlier, intangible in nature. However, associating our sixth mental hook, *chow* (for which we picture a big cereal bowl), with magazine is not difficult at all. Simply picture yourself eating chow from this gigantic bowl, and all of a sudden you realize you are eating a shredded magazine. Or a thousand gigantic magazines suddenly come shooting out of your bowl of chow. Or you spill your chow all over your magazine. You learned earlier how to make the associations. Now it is only a matter of knowing what to associate with what, and the hooks take care of that for you.

Let's do another example. The eighth item on that list was *soccer ball.* The Mental Hook for 8 is *foe.* Associate your foe with a soccer ball and you will have it locked in your mental filing cabinet. How you make the association is up to you. You could see your foe slipping as he or she tries to kick the soccer ball. Or your foe gets hit with thousands and thousands of gigantic soccer balls. Or he/she kicks the winning goal past the goalie, which happens to be you. Make the association any way you want. I would strongly suggest, however, that you use one or more of the six methods of Imagination-Association that we also learned in Chapter 2. Let's do one more example.

The third item on our list was car. The Mental Hook for number 3 is *ma.* For this association, I'm going to simply picture my ma driving the biggest, most beautiful car in the world, and does she look great driving it! Make up your own association between your ma and car, and you will have it mentally filed.

Now if I ask you what the sixth item on my list was, and you know that the sixth mental hook is *chow,* how would you respond? Sure, *magazine,* because you can see that association. What was the eighth item on that list, the eighth Mental Hook being *foe*? That's right, you could see that association between *soccer ball* and your *foe*. And knowing that the third Mental Hook is *ma*, what was the third item on the list? "Car," because you made that association correctly. The good news is that it also works in reverse. For instance, again assuming that you know your Mental Hooks, what number on the list was magazine? And soccer ball? And what about car? If you know your Hooks, you know the answer.

This Will Seem Amazing!

Now, I'm going to give you a brand new list of twenty items. Since you haven't taken the time to memorize your first twenty Mental Hooks, I will put them in bold letters next to their numbers. Please glance at the list quickly, without making the associations, and then read on.

1.	**Toe**—Pliers	11.	**Toad**—Pencil sharpener
2.	**Noah**—Shopping cart	12.	**Tin**—Wristwatch
3.	**Ma**—Telephone	13.	**Tam**—Playing cards
4.	**Row**—Rabbits	14.	**Tree**—Ice cream cones
5.	**Law**—Oranges	15.	**Towel**—James Buchanan
6.	**Chow**—Staples	16.	**Teach**—Ironing board
7.	**Cow**—Judge	17.	**Tag**—Rock
8.	**Foe**—Book	18.	**Taffy**—Sailboat
9.	**Boy**—Computer	19.	**Tub**—Trophy
10.	**Ties**—Black Paint	20.	**Nose**—Pipe

Let's go through the list one by one, locking each item into our mental filing cabinet as we progress. You need to make sure you **see** and even **feel** each association, even if it's just for a split second. Merely reading it like a novel will not work. I will supply you with suggested associations solely for additional ideas in case you feel stuck. However, if you think an association that you make on your own works better, then please go ahead and use it.

1. **Toe**—Pliers: Picture yourself taking a pair of pliers and squeezing your big toe with them, until you can tear your toe off. A gruesome association; however, if you can see it and feel it, you will remember it.

2. **Noah**—Shopping cart: Picture Noah needing a gigantic shopping cart in order to buy the tremendous amount of food necessary to feed all the animals and people living on his ark. Poor ol' Noah is pushing this shopping cart which is at least ten times bigger than he is!

3. **Ma**—Telephone: Picture your ma having a great time talking on the telephone with her sister or grandchild whom she hasn't seen in a long, long time.

4. **Row**—Rabbits: Knowing how incredibly fast rabbits can multiply, let's picture a row of dirt in a garden miles and miles long, and one by one, hundreds and hundreds and maybe even thousands of rabbits are popping their heads out of the ground.

5. **Law**—Oranges: The burglar is rummaging around through your home while you are asleep. As you wake up, you notice that your police (law) officer takes out his gun, and shoots the burglar. Instead of bullets coming out of the gun, however, out come giant oranges. They hit the burglar right in the mouth, and the burglar looks real dumb with an orange sticking out of his mouth.

6. **Chow**—Staples: Business just hasn't been that good lately, and the only thing you can afford to eat for chow tonight are the staples in your desk drawer. Take them out of their box and pour them into your bowl. Now take a bite. Yech!

7. **Cow**—Judge: This one's a real silly picture. You have had your day in court, and the judge is about to pronounce the verdict. Only this judge turns out to be a cow. See that judge, who is really a cow wearing the gown and wig, slamming down her gavel and yelling, "MOOOOOO!"

8. **Foe**—Book: Wouldn't it just really burn your gut to see a picture of your foe's ugly face on the cover of a book that he/she has authored? It would me. (Come to think of it, I wonder if that's how my foe felt when he picked up this book.)

9. **Boy**—Computer: Imagine buying your boy a beautiful new computer. You tell him not to play with it before he learns how to use it properly. Unfortunately, he doesn't listen this time, and as soon as you walk away he starts playing with it and destroys the entire machine. Hello, MasterCard.

10. **Ties**—Black Paint: In this picture the guy walks down the stairs to ask his date which of the three brand-new ties around his neck goes best with his suit. The woman, who happens to have a bucket of black paint in her hand, steps towards him in order to take a closer look. As she does, she spills that bucket of black paint all over those brand new ties. Oh no!...What a mess!

11. **Toad**—Pencil sharpener: For this association, picture sticking the leg of a live toad inside a pencil sharpener. Do not! I repeat, do not turn the handle! (Again, if you are an animal lover as I am, realize that this is only make-believe, and the toad is not getting hurt.)

12. **Tin**—Wristwatch: Imagine you have just bought a beautiful new wristwatch. You are so protective of this wristwatch, however, that you cover it with tinfoil every time you go out. One day, as you remove the tinfoil, you see that the foil has marked up and destroyed the face of the watch. Hello, Visa.

13. **Tam**—Playing cards: In this scenario, see yourself dealing thousands and thousands and thousands of playing cards, quick as can be. All of a sudden you feel your wrist and arm getting heavier and heavier. You look at the cards to see why and you realize that the playing cards have turned into gigantic orange tams.

14. **Tree**—Ice cream cones: As hot as it is outside (if it isn't, then imagine it), you would sure love an ice cream cone. Unfortunately you have no money, and ice cream cones don't grow on trees. In this case, however, they do. Walk over to your tree and see all those beautiful, delicious-looking ice cream cones just begging you to come over and take one.

15. **Towel**—James Buchanan: I put him at number 15 for two reasons. One, he was the fifteenth president of the United States of America, and two, we will once again need to employ a Soundalike, as we did in Chapter 2 when we remembered presidents 11 through 20 in sequence. This time, however, we are going to associate Buchanan with the fifteenth Mental Hook, which is *towel*. How? First, our Soundalike for Buchanan was *two cannons*. Two cannons can be easily pictured, and it sounds enough like Buchanan to remind us of the correct word. Imagine how dirty two cannons can get. They can become so dirty, in fact, that you would need a huge towel in order to clean them. See yourself taking this huge towel and sweating profusely as you clean out those two cannons. Two cannons should remind you of Buchanan.

16. **Teach**—Ironing board: In your mind's eye, see your teacher having to grade so much homework at home, that there is no time for ironing there. Instead, your teacher must bring his/her ironing to school to get it done. See that ironing board smack dab in the middle of the classroom, sticking out like a sore thumb. That'll teach your teacher to give you so much homework!

17. **Tag**—Rock: Most rocks do not have any monetary value, but the one you have in your hand does. There is a gigantic price tag on it, and it says $1,000,000.

18. **Taffy**—Sailboat: Picture your sailboat getting caught in a taffy storm. After the storm is over, it won't move because the masts are covered with gooey, sticky taffy. (However, it tastes great!)

19. **Tub**—Trophy: You have just won the biggest trophy of your life. It is so big, in fact, that the only place in your entire home where it will fit is your bathtub. Picture your trophy relaxing, taking a hot bath in the tub.

20. **Nose**—Pipe: In your mind's eye, see yourself smoking a pipe, through your nose. Inhale...ARGHHHHH!

Let's Put It To The Test

Now it is time to test ourselves and see how we did. I will give you the number and Mental Hook, and you fill in the blank with the correct item. Don't panic! Look at the hook and try to remember the association. If you are having trouble with one, skip it for the moment, fill in the rest, and then go back to it. We will be doing this out of sequence, so you will see just how truly amazing this system is. Go ahead, and good luck.

8.	Foe_____	3.	Ma _____
14.	Tree_____	17.	Tag _____
2.	Noah _____	11.	Toad _____
19.	Tub _____	5.	Law _____
15.	Towel _____	18.	Taffy _____
4.	Row _____	9.	Boy _____
20.	Nose _____	13.	Tam _____
7.	Cow _____	16.	Teach _____
1.	Toe _____	10.	Ties _____
12.	Tin _____	6.	Chow_____

Well, how did you do? I bet you got most of them. And you did it out of sequence as well. And it will work in reverse as well. Watch this....

Judge_____	Staples _____
Sailboat_____	Telephone _____
Oranges_____	Pencil sharpener_____
Wristwatch _____	Trophy _____
Book _____	Shopping cart_____
Playing cards _____	Black paint_____
Ironing board _____	James Buchanan _____
Ice cream cones _____	Rock_____
Pliers_____	Rabbits_____
Computer _____	Pipe _____

If you have already committed your first 20 Mental Hooks to memory, then you can simply fill in the number next to the appropriate item. If you haven't, then write down the hook you associated with that item, and then check your list of Mental Hooks to find the number, or use your knowledge of the Mnemonic Alphabet to help you figure out the correct number. You can do that with any list of 20 for the rest of your life, so long as you know the first 20 Mental Hooks by memory. Naturally, you will not be able to carry around these hooks; you must have them permanently fixed in your mental filing cabinet. Pretty amazing, isn't it?

Now you might be asking; "Well Bob, having the ability to remember lists in and out of sequence is somewhat important, but not *that* important! Is that all the Mental Hooks are good for?" NO WAY! That is just the tip of the iceberg. Knowledge of the following 100 Mental Hooks will give you the ability to easily remember facts, dates, telephone numbers, addresses, appointments, and much, much more. Stay tuned for a life-changing experience.

It Isn't Even Difficult

Meanwhile, what about committing the remaining 80 hooks to memory? Here is how we do it. First, quickly glance through the hooks and notice again that they must all fit in with the rules dictated by our Mnemonic Alphabet: beginning and ending consonant sounds must equal the correct number. They are also all tangible, distinct and separate from one another. As you go through the list, if some of them just don't cut it for you, change them to something else, so long as it meets the criteria.

Mental Hooks 21-100

21.	Nut	35.	Mule	49.	Rope	63.	Jam	76.	Cash	90.	Base
22.	Nun	36.	Match	50.	Lease	64.	Chair	77.	Cake	91.	Boat
23.	Name	37.	Mike	51.	Light	65.	Jail	78.	Cuff	92.	Bone
24.	Nero	38.	Muff	52.	Lion	66.	Choo-	79.	Cup	93.	Bomb
25.	Nail	39.	Map	53.	Lime		Choo	80.	Face	94.	Bear
26.	Niche	40.	Rose	54.	Lawyer	67.	Check	81.	Foot	95.	Bell
27.	Nook	41.	Rat	55.	Lily	68.	Chief	82.	Fin	96.	Beach
28.	Navy	42.	Rain	56.	Lodge	69.	Ship	83.	Foam	97.	Bag
29.	Nap	43.	Room	57.	Lake	70.	Case	84.	Fire	98.	Puff
30.	Mouse	44.	Rear	58.	Leaf	71.	Coat	85.	File	99.	Pipe
31.	Meat	45.	Rail	59.	Lob	72.	Cane	86.	Fish	100.	Disease
32.	Moon	46.	Roach	60.	Cheese	73.	Comb	87.	Fig		
33.	Mummy	47.	Rake	61.	Chute	74.	Core	88.	Fife		
34.	Mower	48.	Roof	62.	Chain	75.	Coal	89.	Fob		

Fun And Simple Drills

There are several different ways to make learning these hooks enjoyable. First, you can cover up the numbers and try to recall the hook (the picture, *not* the word). If you get stuck, just think of the correct consonant sounds and fill in the rest of the hook with vowels. For instance, for number 52, you know it must contain both the "luh" sound for 5, and the "nuh" sound for 2. Fill in the rest with vowels. Is it lane, lean, line, lion, loan? Well, in my case it is lion. Do this a few times and you will get faster and faster.

Next, you can make up little flash cards like I did, and carry them around with you wherever you go. You would be surprised how much time is usually wasted sitting around waiting for meetings when you could be turning that wasted time into productive time. How about while you are eating, or drinking coffee, or waiting at the doctor's office, or at a red light (definitely *not* during a green light)? You could have a spouse or child or parent or friend quiz you, and make you respond just a bit quicker each time. And you could even record the hooks on your tape recorder and listen to them in your car on your way to work. Talk about time management!

Just A Bit Of Work Will Be Greatly Rewarded

To do these practice exercises you absolutely must know your Mnemonic Alphabet by heart, and be willing to put just a relatively little bit of effort into something that will pay big dividends many times over. And if they aren't coming to you at the snap of a finger at first, don't sweat it. As I mentioned earlier, you only have to know them in a reasonable period of time. And besides, day by day you will get faster until one day, when you hear a number, you will automatically picture the correct Mental Hook, and you will say to yourself, "Hey, I know these!" And please keep in mind, it is not important to see the word, but the picture. Congratulations. It gets real fun from here on in.

"Hell begins on the day we gain a clear vision of all that we might have achieved, of all the gifts we have wasted, of all that we might have done which we did not do."

Gian-Carlo Menotti

*C*HAPTER 9

Learn And Remember
Our Presidents

"Nothing is really work unless you would rather be doing something else."

James Barrie

Throughout this nation's history, our presidents have played an extremely important role in its functioning, growth, history and international perception. Being the president is probably the most important, as well as the most powerful, position that one can assume. Yet most of us don't know the names of the 41 men who have held that office, and I guarantee you, very, very few people know them in and out of numerical sequence. However, using our Mental Hooks, we can learn just that in a relatively small amount of time. As we go through the list, I will suggest the associations, but if you feel that another association will work even better, then of course I want you to go right ahead and use it.

In this exercise, we are going to lock in only the last name of each president. Many of us can recall the first names, once we are reminded by hearing the last names. If you would also like to put the first name to memory, you can easily employ the Chain Link Method you utilized in the chapter on names and faces.

1. **Toe**—Washington (wash a ton): See your toe working hard trying to wash a ton. A ton of what? I picture a block weighing 2000 pounds. Washing a ton.

2. **Noah**—Adams (atom bomb): Picture the Atom Bomb exploding on Noah's Ark.

3. **Ma**—Jefferson (chef for son): Most mothers will probably tell you that this association is an easy one. Just say to yourself, "Mothers often seem to be a 'chef for (their) son'."

4. **Row**—Madison (mad at sun): During a drought, a row in a garden would definitely be "mad at the sun" for drying out and killing its plants and flowers.

5. **Law**—Monroe (man row): Imagine a criminal trying to get away from a law officer by jumping into a boat. See this "man row" the boat as fast as he can while the law officer is chasing him.

6. **Chow**—Adams (atom bomb): Picture yourself chowing on an Atom Bomb and it explodes. Not a pretty picture, is it? But it will probably work.

7. **Cow**—Jackson (jacks, sun): Imagine thousands of toy jacks coming out of a cow's udders instead of milk because the sun is so hot.

8. **Foe**—Van Buren (van, bureau): See your foe stealing your van, which contains your most expensive bureau. You give chase, but to no avail.

9. **Boy**—Harrison (hairy son): Picture your boy with a beard. He is a very "hairy son."

10. **Ties**—Tyler (tie): Just the fact that this president's name has a "tie" right in it makes it easy to remember. Just be careful. Sometimes the real simple ones are the most difficult to remember.

11. **Toad**—Polk (poke): See yourself poke a hole through a toad's tummy with your index finger. Again, not pretty, but it will probably work.

12. **Tin**—Taylor (taylor): Imagine a tailor using a needle and thread made entirely of tin.

13. **Tam**—Fillmore (fill more): In your mind's eye, see yourself attempt to "fill more" of that tam with whatever you desire.

14. **Tree**—Pierce (pears): Again, this one is almost too logical, so be as imaginative as possible. For instance, see a tree filled with

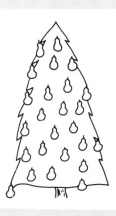

thousands and thousands of gigantic pears. (**Note:** even though in Chapter 2, I used *pierced*, as in pierced ears, as a Soundalike for President Pierce, I used *pears* for this example because it was even easier to lock in.)

15. **Towel**—Buchanan (two cannons): It's hard work to clean two cannons, so you will probably need an awfully big towel.

16. **Teach**—Lincoln: Since most of us are already familiar with President Lincoln and can picture him, simply imagine your teacher trying to teach you all about Lincoln.

17. **Tag**—Johnson (yawn, sun): In your mind's eye, picture a tremendous "yawn" from the "sun," as you place a gigantic price tag on it.

18. **Taffy**—Grant (as in allow): Say to yourself, as you picture, "Will they 'grant' us the right to eat as much taffy as we want?"

19. **Tub**—Hayes (haze): Imagine that your bathtub is filled with "haze."

20. **Nose**—Garfield (cigar, field): Picture yourself using your nose in order to plant a bunch of "cigars" in a "field."

21. **Nut**—Arthur (art, as in artist): See this artist drawing the most perfect picture of a chestnut imaginable. That automatically locks in his first name, which was Chester.

22. **Nun**—Cleveland: We can simply associate a Catholic nun with the city of Cleveland. She definitely wants to be transferred out of Cleveland. (If you happen to be one of my many friends from Cleveland, please don't feel that this was just another bad "Cleveland" joke. If it had been any other city, I would have used the same type of association.)

23. **Name**—Harrison (hairy son): Imagine that your son is so hairy that he needs a "name" tag to identify him.

24. **Nero**—Cleveland: You may recall from your history books that Nero was the man who fiddled while Rome burned to the ground. In this case though, we are going to imagine him, complete with toga, fiddling while the city of Cleveland burns to the ground.

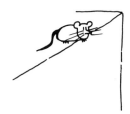

25. **Nail**—McKinley (my can leak): If you stick a nail in my can of soup, I would probably say "Watch 'my can leak.'"

26. **Niche**—Roosevelt (loose felt): Picture yourself completely filling up a niche in the ground with "loose felt."

27. **Nook**—Taft (taffy): See the taffy you are cooking explode all over the kitchen nook. The nook is just covered with hot, gooey, sticky taffy.

28. **Navy**—Wilson (will, sun): Picture in your mind's eye that everyone in the Navy writes out a "will" in case they get too much "sun."

29. **Nap**—Harding (hard ink): Imagine how difficult it would be to take a nap while somebody is squirting you with "hard ink."

30. **Mouse**—Coolidge (cool, ledge): See a mouse on a ledge high above the ground. Let's hope that mouse can keep its "cool" on that "ledge" so as not to fall off.

31. **Meat**—Hoover (vacuum): Picture a huge Hoover™ vacuum cleaner cleaning the dirt off a piece of meat.

32. **Moon**—Roosevelt (loose felt): In your mind's eye, look at the moon. What is it made out of? You guessed it! "Loose felt."

33. **Mummy**—Truman (true man): as you see this picture, say to yourself, "A 'true man' would never be afraid of one of those Egyptian mummies."

34. **Mower**—Eisenhower (hour glass): Imagine that it should take less than an hour to mow your lawn. See yourself turning over the "hour" glass so you will know for sure.

35. **Mule**—Kennedy (can of tees): This particular mule loves to golf. See him going to the golf shop to buy a "can of tees."

36. **Match**—Johnson (yawn, sun): Make believe that millions of miles up in the sky, the "sun" gets tired and begins to "yawn" whenever someone lights a match.

37. **Mike**—Nixon: For President Nixon I don't believe we need a Soundalike. Just remember that it was what he said into a "mike," or microphone, that contributed to the downfall of this former president.

38. **Muff**—Ford (car): Picture that this car, which of course is a Ford, gets cold very easily while being driven, and wears its favorite muffs.

39. **Map**—Carter (car tear): Imagine yourself driving your car over a map. Watch that "car tear" that map into thousands of little pieces!

40. **Rose**—Reagan (ray gun): In your mind's eye, picture yourself shooting at a rose with your new "ray gun."

41. **Rat**—Bush (bush): Imagine that hiding behind the "bush" is a gigantic rat.

Now let's quiz ourselves. Actually, first just run through the associations one more time, making sure you have them. Then move on to the quiz. I will give you the numbers with their hooks beside them. (Although by now you should be well on your way to knowing the first 40 or 50 hooks by heart.) If you were able to effectively make the association, you should get the correct president.

Remember, the process also works in reverse. So as long as you know your first 41 hooks, you can hear the president's name and automatically know which number president he was.

The way to really make this list true knowledge is to review every so often. Think of a number between 1 and 41, and the correct president should come to mind. Similarly, when you hear a president's name, the correct number should come to you. After several of these reviews, you will have all that information locked in your mind forever.

5.	(Law) _____	25.	(Nail) _____
16.	(Teach) _____	34.	(Mower) _____
9.	(Boy) _____	12.	(Tin) _____
30.	(Mouse) _____	22.	(Nun) _____
38.	(Muff) _____	1.	(Toe) _____
20.	(Nose) _____	35.	(Mule) _____
17.	(Tag) _____	32.	(Moon) _____
13.	(Tam) _____	3.	(Ma) _____
28.	(Navy) _____	10.	(Ties) _____
41.	(Rat) _____	21.	(Nut) _____
8.	(Foe) _____	7.	(Cow) _____
27.	(Nook) _____	23.	(Name) _____
31.	(Meat) _____	6.	(Chow) _____
4.	(Row) _____	40.	(Rose) _____
36.	(Match) _____	24.	(Nero) _____
29.	(Nap) _____	39.	(Map) _____
2.	(Noah) _____	26.	(Niche) _____
14.	(Tree) _____	18.	(Taffy) _____
37.	(Mike) _____	19.	(Tub) _____
11.	(Toad) _____	15.	(Towel) _____
20.	(Nose) _____		

CHAPTER 10

American Facts, People And History

Remembering the people, events and important facts that make up our country's rich heritage can be both easy and a lot of fun when using this system. Let's put our knowledge of the Link System, Soundalike, Mnemonic Alphabet and Mental Hooks to use during this chapter as we take a look at Americana. I will give you the questions, answers, and suggestions for locking the answers in (however, I would rather you try making your own associations), and then follow with a quiz.

Who was the first American woman to win the Nobel Peace Prize, and in what year? Jane Addams, 1931. I would put it to memory this way. A good picture or Soundalike for the name Addams is *atom*, as in the Atom Bomb. We can very well imagine that Jane Addams was certainly not awarded the Nobel Peace Prize for inventing the Atom Bomb. No way! That should help us to remember her name, which is Addams. Now, how about the year in which she won it, 1931? First, we would break the year 1931 into two separate hooks, 19 being *tub* and 31 being *meat.* Using the Chain Link system, we first link together Jane Addams, which we already know, with tub (19). Let's imagine that Ms. Addams felt so proud of herself after being awarded the Nobel Peace Prize that she decided to reward herself by taking a nice warm bubblebath in her tub. Now let's link tub with meat (31). Now she is going all out with her self-reward. Not only is she enjoying a hot bubblebath in her tub, but she also has someone serving her the most delicious piece of steak, or meat, while she is in the tub. Now we know that

the first American woman to win the Nobel Peace Prize was Jane Addams, and she accomplished this feat in the year 1931.

Incidentally, I would like to take this opportunity to point out that you use only what is necessary to successfully put the desired information to memory. For instance, if you already know that Ms. Addams was awarded the Nobel Peace Prize in the 1900s, you would not have to include "tub," the hook for 19 in your chain link. You would simply link together Jane Addams with "meat," for 31.

Next, how many acres are covered by the Pentagon? The answer is 34. How would we remember that?

> First, we know that our Mental Hook for 34 is *mower,* as in lawn mower. Simply incorporate that into your picture by imagining how difficult it would be to take a lawn mower and mow all the land covered by the Pentagon. You might see yourself sweating, huffing and puffing as you try to push your gigantic lawn mower throughout the Pentagon.

Of what metal is the Statue of Liberty made?

> Copper. In order to remember that, I might make things tangible by seeing copper represented by a bunch of police officers, or cops. In fact, see thousands and thousands of cops building the Statue of Liberty. Cops should remind you of the answer, which is copper.

Time For A Soundalike

In what state is the geyser Old Faithful?

> The answer is Wyoming. Now this could be a tough bit of information to lock in, because ordinarily the word *Wyoming* would be difficult to picture. But not in this case, because we have the Soundalike. For Wyoming, a workable Soundalike might be, *why a mink?* Doesn't *why a mink* sound enough like Wyoming to serve as a good reminder of the true word? Sure it does!
>
> Now, we just need to associate it with the geyser Old Faithful. Picture a man handing his wife a beautiful mink stole. His

wife is surprised, but delighted. She asks him, "Darling, why a mink?" To which the man responds, "Because to me, you are old faithful." Yes, that may seem awfully silly, but you know by now that it will probably work when it comes time to test your memory.

How many judges are there in the Supreme Court?

Nine. We know our Mental Hook for the number 9 is our standard *boy*. Look one-by-one down the bench of the Supreme Court and get a vivid picture of your boy being every one of the judges. See him wearing the robe, and everything else that would make that ridiculous and humorous picture clear to you.

In what year was President Harry S. Truman born? 1884.

The first thing we have to do is either picture President Truman, or, if we don't know what he looked like, come up with a Soundalike for Truman. Since many readers likely are too young to remember President Truman, let's use a Soundalike for his name. How about *true man? True man* should certainly serve as a good enough reminder for Truman.

Now we need to come up with Mental Hooks for the year 1884. However, I am going to assume that we all know that President Truman would have to have been born in 1884 as opposed to 1984. Because of that, let's not bother putting *taffy* (18) into the picture, but go right to *fire* (84). Now let's successfully link together true man and fire. You might say to yourself, as you see this picture, "A true man would always put out a fire."

Now that is another fairly ridiculous sentence and picture, but I bet it will prove effective. Notice how we use only what is necessary in order to make this system work?

Who was the poet who read at the inauguration of President John F. Kennedy?

I'll tell you what, if you can picture in your mind's eye that on that particular day there happened to be a chilling *frost*, then you can remember that the poet was Robert Frost.

In what year did astronaut Neil Armstrong set foot on the moon? The answer is 1969.

I am going to once again assume that we all know it was 1969 as opposed to 1869, so let's go right to the Mental Hook for 69, which is *ship*, and maybe picture Armstrong landing a real ship, or a huge battleship on the moon.

If you need to remind yourself that the astronaut's name is Armstrong, fine. See a picture of a very muscular (strong) arm landing a huge battleship on the moon by using its muscles to somehow accomplish this feat safely. Please remember to **use your imagination!**

In what year did Alexander Graham Bell invent the telephone? 1876.

In this case I am going to assume that most of us know that it was in fact Dr. Bell who invented the phone, but I won't assume that we know in which century his invention took place.

Therefore, we need to come up with two hooks for the year 1876. Those hooks would be *taffy* (18) and *cash* (76).

The way I locked this in was to see him inventing a telephone made entirely out of hot, sticky, gooey, yet delicious taffy. And, of course, this taffy telephone was such a great invention that Dr. Bell made mucho cash from it. Taffy and cash will give us 1876.

Of course, if you already knew that this invention took place in the 1800s, you would merely associate Dr. Bell with cash.

Who invented the Cotton Gin, and in what year?

Eli Whitney in 1793. First, let's associate Cotton Gin, which we already know, with Eli Whitney, which we want to remember. Actually, we will associate Cotton Gin with only the last name, Whitney. We learned in the chapter on names and faces how to lock in first names with last names. For now, Whitney will be fine.

One picture might be to see yourself pouring gallons of gin into a lone cotton ball. That would represent Cotton Gin. Now

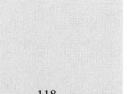

rub this cotton filled with gin (cotton gin) all over your knee, turning it bright white. *White knee* will serve as a Soundalike for Whitney. Now we know that Whitney invented the Cotton Gin.

It is time to associate Whitney with 1793, the two hooks being *tag* and *bomb*. We could do this one of two ways. The first would be to associate white knee with tag and then bomb. But I would be more inclined to simply associate a picture of a Cotton Gin, which is easily pictured, with tag, and then bomb.

For instance, since the Cotton Gin would so heavily impact the cotton industry, I would see this Cotton Gin having a tremendously huge price tag (17) on it. However, somebody might have been awfully jealous, and planted a bomb (93) right underneath that huge tag. See the Cotton Gin exploding because of the bomb placed under the tag, and you will remember that the Cotton Gin was invented by Eli Whitney in the year 1793.

In what Texas city did a terrible hurricane occur, killing over 6000 people, and in what year?

The answers to these questions are Galveston and 1900. First, we know we must come up with a Soundalike for Galveston. How about *call fist in. Call fist in* will remind us of Galveston, won't it? Let's form the crazy association of imagining the people *call*ing their *fist in* (call fist in) when the hurricane began, so that their fist would not get caught in the hurricane. Now that's heavy duty weird imagining there, but so what? It will work just fine.

Now we need to work into our story the hooks for 1900, which are *tub* and *sauce*. We might see the people taking their fist, which they just called in, and throwing it into the tub (19), and then pouring hot spaghetti sauce (00) on it to keep it safe. Why, I don't know, but it should be very easy to picture.

How many states are physically touched by the Mississippi River?

Ten. This one will be real easy. Picture throwing a bunch of gigantic, multi-colored *ties,* our hook for 10, into the Mississippi River. Each time the Mississippi River reaches into another state, one of the ties jumps out and onto the land.

In what year did the United States complete the Panama Canal?

> 1914. Let's again assume that we know the date was in the twentieth century, thus we need only to associate the Mental Hook *tree* (14) with the Panama Canal.
>
> We might see those workers on the isthmus being so elated that their job was finally over that they planted thousands and thousands of gigantic trees from one end of the Panama Canal to the other, in order to celebrate.

In what year was oil discovered in Texas?

> The answer is 1901. Again, we will simply associate oil with *suit*, which we'll use as our Mental Hook for 01. See those wildcatters out there trying to discover oil while wearing their best new suits. When the oil shoots up out of the ground, it gets all over their new suits. That should remind us of the correct answer.
>
> One quick note at this point: Even though the picture is a bit silly because people drilling for oil certainly would not be wearing their best suits while drilling was taking place, the picture of oil getting all over their new suits is still almost too logical. It's the logical ones that are often the most difficult to remember. Because of that, make sure to go out of your way to make that picture as shocking and illogical as possible.

And finally, in what year did the Titanic sink?

> 1912. Again, we would know that the Titanic sank during this century, so we don't need to put *tub* (19) into our Chain Link. Instead, simply associate the Titanic with *tin*, the Mental Hook for 12. You might see the Titanic sinking because it was made of tin foil, which certainly could not withstand hitting an iceberg.

All right, it is time to test our memory of the information we have studied in this chapter. I will give you the question followed by a blank space for you to fill in. Don't try to come up with the answer right away, only the association. Once you remember the association, you will then remember the answer. Do the best you can, and then look back to check the answers.

Now, go back to the beginning of this chapter and check your answers. I bet that you got most of them correct. If you did, then great! If not, just go back over the questions that gave you a problem, and be sure to make a clear, concrete, and illogical association.

Again, this system is not magic, and most of us won't bat 1000 every time. However, at this point I am sure you can see just how much easier and more fun it can make learning any material. If you are an adult reading this, can't you just imagine how much easier it would have been to learn facts, dates, and other information in school had you known about this system and put it to use back then?

And just as importantly, if you *are* a student at this time, whether in Junior High School, High School, College or Night School, please don't just *imagine* how useful this can be, use it. Yes, you will still have to put in time studying, but definitely not as much as you would without this system, and the information will stay with you for a much longer period of time.

Who was the first American woman to win the Nobel Peace Prize?

_____

And in what year?_____

How many acres of land are covered by the Pentagon?

_____

Of what metal is the Statue of Liberty made?

_____

In what state is the geyser Old Faithful?

_____

How many judges are there on the Supreme Court?

_____

In what year was President Harry S. Truman born?

_____

Who was the poet who read at the inauguration of John F. Kennedy?

_____

In what year did astronaut Neil Armstrong set foot on the moon?

_____

In what year did Alexander Graham Bell invent the telephone?

_____

Who invented the Cotton Gin?

_____

And in what year?_____

In what Texas city did a terrible hurricane occur, killing over 6000 people?

_____

And in what year?_____

How many states are physically touched by the Mississippi River?

_____

In what year did the United States complete the Panama Canal?

_____

In what year was oil discovered in Texas?

_____

In what year did the Titanic sink?

_____

Alphabet Soundalikes And Hooks

Now let's take a look at something you'll find simple and quite easy to learn, but that will come in handy time and again. Alphabet Soundalikes and Alphabet Hooks serve several purposes: as Soundalikes for names or parts of names; as 26 additional Mental Hooks for those times when you need different, or extra, hooks; as hooks to file items by letter instead of number; and for remembering style or serial numbers containing letters.

Difficult To Picture

Please keep in mind that letters, just like numbers, are basically intangible. They have no rhyme or reason to them, but are merely geometrical shapes and designs to which we give labels, or names. What this entire book is really all about is allowing us to picture items that normally cannot be seen or pictured, because once we can picture something and see it in our mind's eye, we can remember it. Think back for a moment to some of the times when you had to remember items that contained either just letters or even a combination of letters and numbers. For instance, license plates, tag items, products, serial numbers, etc.

Don't Panic! These Are Easy!

What you will learn in this chapter will show you how to take all letters, those normally intangible items, and work with them as you would with anything else that you can picture.

"So how do we picture letters?" Easy. We simply put a picture of something in their places. "But Bob, does that mean we're going to have to sit down and memorize pictures, or hooks, for the 26 different letters of the entire alphabet?" Watch this! It won't be difficult at all. And we'll see by going down the list that they all make perfect sense.

Let's Do The First Two Together

For instance, for the letter *A*, the picture we would use is *ape*. Why? For two reasons: one, an ape is a lot more tangible, or easy to picture, than the letter *A*, and two, ape sounds like *A*. As you can see, that isn't something you have to spend a lot of time putting to memory.

B is the next letter. The picture we use for the letter *B* is the insect *Bee*. Again, bee, the insect, is certainly much easier to picture than the letter *B*, and bee not only sounds a lot like the letter *B*, it sounds *exactly* like the letter *B*.

The pattern of the first two letters continues the entire way through the alphabet.

A—ape	J—jaybird	S—asp
B—bee	K—cape	T—tea (cup of)
C—sea, seal	L—elf	U—ewe
D—tee (golf)	M—M & Ms™	V—veal
E—eel	N—ant	W—double goo
F—off (light switch)	O—Cheerios™	X—eggs
G—jeans	P—pea	Y—wine
H—itch	Q—cue stick	Z—zebra
I—eye	R—hour (glass)	

First Example: A Television Set

Now let's practice in a lifelike situation. You need to remember the serial or style number of a television set you want to buy, or possibly compare. For one reason or another, you cannot write this information down on paper, so you must memorize it. The serial number of the television set happens to be 20A537XNY. Fine, let's do it.

First, we must associate that which we know with what we wish to remember. We know *television set;* the serial number is what we wish to remember. So, let's break up that serial number into pictures the way we have learned. The number 20 would be *nose.* A is *ape,* 53 would be *lime,* 7 is *cow,* for X we would picture *eggs,* N would be *ant,* and Y would be represented by *wine.*

The beginning association would be *television set* to *nose.* Again, for this example I will make the associations, but of course you're welcome to use your own instead. And, as is the case with everything else we have done, the more of these you do and the more you practice, the easier it will become, in both speed and effectiveness.

So we have to associate *television set* with *nose* (20). There are many ways we could do this, but in this case let's imagine a television set falling out of your nose. That might be kind of gross, but I think it will work. We now go from *nose* to *ape* (A). Well, that ape was so angry at you for letting that television fall out of your nose that he punched you right in the nose, and I'll bet that hurt. Next we have *lime* (53). In order to make your nose stop hurting, you took thousands and thousands of gigantic, juicy limes and rubbed them on your nose, as though that would help, but it didn't. The next picture is *cow* (7). In order to associate lime with cow, let's picture thousands and thousands of gigantic limes coming out of the cow's udders instead of milk. Talk about sour milk! The next association is with *eggs* (X). Hmm, let's picture taking those limes, putting them over a hot skillet, tapping their sides on the skillet, and seeing them open up like eggs. Picture all the yolks coming out and forming fried eggs. That's substitution, isn't it? From eggs we go to *ant* (N). And guess what the very favorite food of this particular ant happens to be? That's right, eggs, especially those with the flavor of lime. In your mind's eye, see that tiny ant trying to eat all those eggs. He's having so much fun he invites his friends to join him. Picture an entire swarm of ants feasting on those eggs. And finally, we go from ant to *wine* (Y). In order to wash down those eggs, our ant and his buddies take an enormous bottle of wine and attempt to drink the entire bottle.

Important To Review

We just completed the entire Chain Link. Now simply run through it in your mind's eye a couple of times, and you'll know it for as long as you want. And even though we would not need to, we could conceivably remember the serial number backwards as well. The longer the serial or item number, the longer the amount of time it will take to put it to memory. But again, imagine how long it would take to put 20A537XNY to memory without the use of this system. Try this with a few more examples that either you make up or someone designs for you. Practice makes almost perfect, and it's a lot of fun.

Contract Information As Well

With regards to filing information by letter, your Alphabet Hooks can simplify matters for you. Let's take, for example, the back of a contract, or a written agreement. The back of this imaginary real estate document contains standards listed from A through W. Let's take a look at them, by individual title. Please note that in our exercise we will not give an explanation of the meaning of each standard, because that is not our purpose here, though it will certainly be easier to commit to memory if you have a background in real estate. Regardless, working through this exercise will serve to illustrate how valuable these Alphabet Hooks can be. Note how fast you can mentally file the following information.

STANDARDS FOR REAL ESTATE TRANSACTIONS

A.	Evidence of title	M.	Special assessment liens
B.	Purchase money mortgage	N.	Inspection, repair and maintenance
C.	Survey	O.	Risk of loss
D.	Termite inspection	P.	Proceeds of sale; closing procedure
E.	Ingress and egress	Q.	Escrow
F.	Leases	R.	Attorney fees; costs
G.	Liens	S.	Failure of performance
H.	Place of closing	T.	Contract not recordable
I.	Time	U.	Conveyance
J.	Documents for closing	V.	Other agreements
K.	Expenses	W.	Warranties
L.	Prorations, credits		

It definitely is *not* an important part of most people's memory-improvement learning process to memorize this entire example. And for the most part, I am going to assume that you know what these terms mean. If you do not know the meaning of a particular term, skip right on past it to one with which you are familiar. Obviously, if you are not familiar with the term, it will be significantly more difficult to put to memory, and I do not want to see you get discouraged when you are not at fault. Only go as far as you wish in this exercise in order to get an idea of how to mentally file by letter. Naturally, if you ever face a similar situation, you will be better prepared if you have had some practice, so seize the opportunity. Again, I will suggest associations for each item, but as I have said about a thousand times already, the imaginative associations you come up with will not only serve you better but also give you that added experience.

A (*ape*)—Evidence of title: Remember the "title" cards from the Monopoly™ game? Just picture a gigantic ape running through your home, destroying everything in its way, as it searches for evidence of one of those title cards in your home.

B (*bee*)—Purchase money mortgage: Our mnemonic bee simply cannot get financing from a lending institution in order to buy that

new beehive he so badly wants, so what does he do? He asks the current owner to hold the note. In other words, he tries to get a purchase money mortgage.

C (*sea*)—Survey: Wouldn't the sea be an awfully strange place to see a surveying company doing a survey? Even so, that's exactly what they're doing. Simply see that strange picture in your mind's eye.

D (*golf tee*)—Termite inspection: See those gigantic wooden tees? The termites would have a field day eating those, wouldn't they?

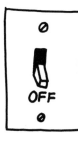

E (*eel*)—Ingress and egress: Ingress and egress mean entrance and exit. Simply picture a slimy ol' eel wiggling his way into the house, all through it, and then back out.

F (*Off (light switch)*)—Leases: In your mind's eye, take a gigantic lease and just stick it on a light switch so hard that the switch tears a hole in the lease.

G (*jeans*)—Liens: See a gigantic pair of starched blue jeans standing at an angle (leaning), not moving at all.

H (*Itch*)—Place of closing: See yourself as the buyer. You are so nervous that when you get to the place of closing, you begin to itch badly.

I (*eye*)—Time: See thousands of gigantic watches coming out of your eyes.

J (*jaybird*)—Documents for closing: Guess who is bringing all those important documents for closing? You got it, our friendly neighborhood jaybird is flying in at this very moment.

K (*cape*)—Expenses: In your mind's eye, see a beautiful cape. You can just imagine how expensive it is.

L (*elf*)—Prorations, credits: Imagine this elf being very confused because being a first time home buyer, our elf has no idea as to what will be prorated and what will be credited. (Again, you would need to be familiar with real estate in order to understand this one.)

M (*M&Ms*™)—Special assessment liens: The public body has put a lien on your M&Ms™ for improvements about to take place on your street.

N (*Ant*)—Inspection, repair and maintenance: See an ant being called in to inspect your future home. This ant knows what needs to be repaired and how much maintenance will be needed. (If you need to help yourself remember the order of those three words, somehow get a woman named Irma (i-r-m) into the picture. Remember "Mnemonic Initialing" in Chapter 3?

O (*Cheerio*)—Risk of loss: Imagine yourself carrying a bunch of Cheerios™ in milk across the kitchen floor on a tiny spoon. You are about to risk losing a Cheerio or two (risk of loss) if you continue to do that.

P (*pea*)—Proceeds of sale, closing procedure: See yourself and the other party dividing up the loot after the close. In this case, the loot is a bunch of giant green peas. Please make sure you abide by the correct procedure.

Q (*cue stick*)—Escrow: For the word *escrow,* let's use the Soundalike "scarecrow." Either picture a scarecrow playing billiards with a cue stick, or see yourself sticking a gigantic cue stick through a scarecrow. Of course, no matter how hard you shove the stick, it won't hurt the scarecrow. (Good thing; he might report you to the wizard, or worse yet, to Dorothy too.)

R (*hour glass*)—Attorney fees, costs: This one is almost too easy. See the attorney turn over the hour glass as the two of you sit down to confer. Those attorney's fees can really cost...or maybe in the long run, they save.

S (*asp*)—Failure of performance: Envision yourself suing that asp (snake) for breaking his promise to sell you his house.

T (*cup of tea*)—Contract not recordable: Someone spilled gallons and gallons of hot tea over that contract. Now we can't make out the words, explaining why this particular contract is not recordable.

U (*ewe*)—Conveyance: For the word, *conveyance,* let's use the Soundalike *conveyor,* as in a conveyor belt. Can't you just picture thousands and thousands of ewes being transported from one place to another on a conveyor belt?

V (*veal*)—Other agreements: Please excuse my personal views getting in the way of this association. In my mind's eye, I see all animal lovers, as well as everyone else, being so disgusted at the inhumane manner in which baby calves are treated that, instead of eating veal, we make other agreements, and that is to boycott veal.

W (*double goo*)—Warranties: See someone putting lots and lots of goo (double goo) over the warranty.

No Pressure, But Give It A Shot

Now go back over these and see how you do. Don't expect to get all of them correct after just one time through, although you will probably remember a surprisingly large number. When you come to one you don't know, redo the association, maybe a bit stronger this time, and then try again.

Review the information a few times, and before long you won't need the associations; the information will become true memory, or true knowledge. Of course, you might not even want to take the time to do it with the previous example. You may instead want to try it with a written agreement you personally need to master. This particular written agreement could be used in the real estate profession. However, this memory system can be adapted to practically any other type of written agreement.

Still Another Application

Let's move on to the next important usage of the Alphabet Soundalikes, and that is as another set of Mental Hooks. At times, depending on the situation, we will need another set of hooks (those things we know) upon which to hang information we want to remember. For instance, you may be in a situation where you must learn several lists in and out of sequence. Well, just in case you begin to get overlap (confusing several different lists on the same Mental Hooks), you can come up with 26 additional hooks. And how is that? Think of it. There are 26 letters in the alphabet, and each one has a numerical position. From *A* being the first letter through *Z* being the twenty-sixth, we have 26 hooks handed right to us. Unfortunately, the majority of us don't know the numerical position for most of the letters. Fortunately, however, we can take care of that right now. Let's line up our first 26 regular Mental Hooks by their proper number, and next to them, their corresponding letters in our alphabet.

1.	Toe—ape	14.	Tree—ant
2.	Noah—bee	15.	Towel—Cheerios™
3.	Ma—sea	16.	Teach—pea
4.	Row—(golf) tee	17.	Tag—cue
5.	Law—eel	18.	Taffy—hour (glass)
6.	Chow—off (light switch)	19.	Tub—asp
7.	Cow—jean	20.	Nose—(cup of) tea
8.	Foe—itch	21.	Nut—ewe
9.	Boy—eye	22.	Nun—veal
10.	Ties—jaybird	23.	Name—double goo
11.	Toad—cape	24.	Nero—eggs
12.	Tin—elf	25.	Nail—wine
13.	Tam—M&Ms™	26.	Niche—zebra

Now what do we do? We simply use our regular Mental Hooks, which we already know, and associate them with our Alphabet Hooks, which we wish to remember. Then go over them in your mind every so often for reinforcement. In a very short period of time, the weird associations will fade because they will no longer be needed. Numerical positions of all 26 letters will become true memory, or true knowledge.

The final advantage (as far as I know) to knowing these Alphabet Soundalikes is that you have the ability to picture letters.

Remember Addresses

The advantages of being able to remember addresses exceed mere convenience. Whether it's the address of someone you know or of a business you need to correspond with or visit, there are instances when having to consult your Rolodex™ wastes time and is aggravating—especially if it's in Phoenix and you're in Boston. With this system, remembering any address is as easy as putting to use the Mnemonic Alphabet, Mental Hooks, Chain Link and Soundalikes.

Let's look at some examples. In each example we are going to follow these steps:

- form a mental picture or Soundalike for either the person's name or the business you wish to remember

- divide the individual numbers into Mental Hooks, or in some cases, simply group more than two numbers together into one picture via the Mnemonic Alphabet

- then come up with a mental picture or Soundalike for the street name

- and finally, link the information for all of these steps together by way of the Chain Link Method. At that point, you will have the option of continuing the link with additional information, when and if it is needed, such as state, zip code, etc.

The first person is Tom Rogers. He lives at 1113 North 58th Street. First, let's take the name Rogers. Does Rogers suggest anything, or do we need a Soundalike? For Rogers, we can picture Mr. Rogers of children's television fame. In the chapter on remembering names and faces I mentioned not using celebrities as mental pictures or Soundalikes for people's names. With addresses (and telephone numbers in the next chapter), that rule does not apply. The reason is that in remembering names and faces, the name is what you want to remember (the person's outstanding facial feature being what you already know). With an address, the name is what you already know (the address being what you want to remember). Confusion is thus avoided. As an aside, I still wouldn't use celebrities too often, but in this case the image will work perfectly with the rest of the Chain Link. For 1113, let's divide that four digit number into two Mental Hooks. 11 is *toad* and 13 is *tam.* For North, we need to picture in our mind's eye a compass. *Compass* is our standard for North. And for 58, the Mental Hook is *leaf.*

Just Link It All Together

Let's take our mental picture of Mr. Rogers and associate, or link it with toad. Picture Mr. Rogers on his T.V. show, but instead of being watched by children, he is being watched by thousands of <u>toad</u>s (11). These toads are each wearing a gigantic orange tam (13). Even though Mr. Rogers is loved by children, let's imagine that the toads cannot stand him. They know they want to get away as fast, and as far, as they can. They need to grab their compasses (North) so they can leap away in the right direction. These toads all attempt to jump on their personal lily pads, but instead of lily pads they turn out to be one gigantic leaf (58). And there you are. Tom Rogers lives at 1113 North 58th Street. Go over that example in your mind's eye several times and you will own that information for as long as needed.

Standards Are Important For Addresses Too

That is how remembering addresses is accomplished. Before the next several examples, I want to give you my standards for the remaining three directions. You already know that for North I picture a compass. For South, I picture a *mouth.* For East, the mental picture of a chunk of *yeast* works just fine, and for West, I suggest picturing either a *pest* or a *vest.* In fact, your vest might even contain a sheriff's star to further remind you of the wild West. For Northeast, Northwest, Southeast, and Southwest, just combine your standards. Many times, of course, you will not have to even bother locking the various directions into your Chain Link. Your natural memory will take care of that for you. However, the standards for directions are there if needed.

The same goes for the difference between streets, roads, places, avenues, lanes, boulevards, etc. Most of the time your natural memory will serve you, but if you want, simply make up standards for those as well. For example, for street you could use *sleet.* For road, *towed,* and you could put a tow truck into your link. For place, a *place mat.* Avenues could be represented by something busy such as *Park Avenue.* For boulevards you could picture *bulls in a yard,* and you could see a *bowling lane* for lanes. Again, you usually will not even need these standards, but they are good to have on hand, just in case.

Next is Dave Marconi, who lives at 69 Staple Street. First take the name Marconi. For that name we could picture *macaroni,* just as we did for his cousin Ed Marconi whom we met in the chapter on names and faces. For 69, the Mental Hook is *ship,* and for staple, just picture a staple. Now link together macaroni with ship (69). Possibly picture in your mind's eye taking a gigantic piece of macaroni and throwing it as hard as you can at a ship. In fact, you throw it so hard that it sticks right to the ship. Now link staple on to that. Even though you are fairly certain that the macaroni will stick to that ship all by itself, you are taking no chances. See yourself taking your gigantic stapler and stapling that piece of macaroni to the ship. Go over that link several times, really making certain to picture it, and you have just locked in Mr. Marconi's address, which is 69 Staple Street.

Multi-Digit Addresses Become A Snap

Our next example is for a business with a fairly lengthy numerical address. As you know by now, it really doesn't matter how many numbers there are. You simply come up with Mental Hooks for every two numbers and just link them together.

The business in this example is Thornapple Chevrolet. It is located at 391612 Zaccariah Place. The first thing to do is decide how to picture Thornapple Chevrolet. Does the name itself present a mental picture or will a Soundalike be needed? One suggestion. Don't make this any more difficult than need be. If Thornapple is the only car dealership whose address you need to commit to memory, simply picture a car. If it is one of several dealerships, but the only Chevrolet dealership, then picturing a particular type of Chevrolet will serve the purpose. If, however, you need to know that it is specifically Thornapple Chevrolet, then take it all the way. For instance, you might see a gigantic, bright red apple with thousands of thorns sticking into it driving a Chevrolet. That would certainly work as a reminder, wouldn't it?

Now you need Mental Hooks to take the place of the numbers 391612. For 39 we have *map*, for 16 we use *teach,* for which we picture our teacher, and for the number 12 there is *tin.* And for the street name, which is Zaccariah, I think it's safe to say we'll definitely need a Soundalike. For Zaccariah, I use *sack of rice*.

All right, we begin with that thorny apple driving the Chevrolet (Thornapple Chevrolet). Now link that to *map* (39). You might see the thorny apple driving your Chevrolet, with you in the passenger's seat, on a gigantic road map, hoping that will help you find the dealership, but it doesn't, and you realize you are lost. Next we have *teach* (16). Fortunately, along the way you spot your teacher hitching a ride. Whether you like that particular teacher or not, you know he/she will be able to teach you how to find the right way. Now link *tin* (12) on to that picture. Your teacher does a strange thing, however. He/she takes out a huge piece of tin foil and begins writing the directions on that tin foil. Unfortunately, the pencil keeps sticking through the tin, which has to be crumpled up. Now that we have 391612, we need to link that to our sack of rice (Zaccariah). Let's use the Imagination-Association technique of substitution. In your mind's eye, see that crumpled tin foil turning into millions and millions of pieces of rice. In fact, so much rice that it must be put into a sack before it fills up your car. Go over that entire scenario several times and it will be yours.

Of course, these stories I'm making up are only meant to show you the method. I would prefer that you make up your own associations. All I ask is that you follow the formula I have given you. Once you feel comfortable with imagery and linking techniques, you can begin making up your own little twists, such as coming up with one or two word-pictures for long numbers that will result in the contrivance of fewer associations. You can convert long-digit numbers to pictures by way of the Mnemonic Alphabet, just as you did at the end of Chapter 7 when you put to memory the social security and checking account numbers.

Let's Cut Out A Step

Would you like to try an example right now using the Mnemonic Alphabet and make up one word-picture instead of using two Mental Hooks? This one's easy. Atlantic Action Limousine is located at 721 Okeechobee Boulevard. Okay, maybe Okeechobee doesn't sound that easy, but I was talking more about the number 721. You see, we could divide that number up into two Mental Hooks, *cane* for 72 and *toe* for 1. Instead, however, let's take the phonetic sounds for 721, "cuh," "nuh" and "tuh," and come up with the word _can't_. Next, for Okeechobee, we need a Soundalike, don't we? Let's use *choke a bee*. That sounds enough like Okeechobee to remind us of the true name. Now we just need to link *can't choke a bee* onto Atlantic Action Limousine, the name we already know and whose address we want to remember. For Atlantic Action Limousine, simply see a limousine. If you elect, you can somehow work Atlantic Action into the picture, possibly seeing it riding over the Atlantic Ocean. Let's associate limousine with "can't choke a bee" by imagining how roomy it is in the back seat of a limousine. In your mind's eye, see a bee bothering you during the ride. You would like to choke this bothersome insect. Unfortunately, the inside of the limousine is so roomy that you can't get near enough to choke it. You can't choke a bee. Can't (721) choke a bee (Okeechobee) is enough to remind you that Atlantic Action Limousine is located at 721 Okeechobee Boulevard.

Let's lock in the address of our new acquaintance, Joanne Butler. She lives at 100 Cherry Street. First take the name Butler. Does that name in itself represent anything picturable? Sure, you can easily picture one of those distinguished-looking English butlers, can't you? For the number 100, the Mental Hook is *disease*. And for Cherry, simply picture a big, red maraschino cherry. You know that first we need to associate our butler with disease. And then link a cherry to that. Picture that distinguished-looking butler suddenly looking very, very sick. It is quite obvious that he has contracted a disease (100). Now link *cherry* to that. It turns out that our butler loves to eat those big red maraschino cherries, but the last one he ate had something wrong with it. It gave him a terrible disease.

Butler, disease and cherry. Sort of a disgusting picture story, but it surely will help you remember that Joanne Butler lives at 100 Cherry Street.

One of your business prospects is Dial Page. They sell pagers. Dial Page is located at 3135 Mapp Road. For the name Dial Page, simply picture a beeper, because that is what it represents. If you have many other prospects who also happen to deal in pagers, you might want to distinguish Dial Page from the others by seeing this particular beeper having a gigantic telephone dial on it. That takes care of that. For the numbers 3135 we just break them up into the Mental Hooks *meat* (31) and *mule* (35). And for Mapp Road a road map will work fine. To begin the Chain Link, first associate *pager* with *meat.* You could see yourself wearing this pager on your belt when all of a sudden it begins to beep. You reach for it, but by the time you shut it off, it turns into a piece of meat (31). Now you might imagine that even though that particular piece of meat is not fit for human consumption, it would be fine to feed to a mule (35). See yourself giving that piece of meat to a mule. In exchange for that piece of meat, the appreciative mule hands you the largest road map (Mapp) you have ever seen. Isn't that simple? Weird, but simple.

Here's An Ideal Example

There is a business in town called Ideal Gifts. They make gift baskets for all occasions. And just in case you *forget* someone's anniversary until the very last minute, you better put that address to memory. The address is 208-4 U.S. Highway One, Suite 42. Let's use this one as an example for practicing locking in dashes and suite numbers. Very easy. As you may have guessed, I have simply made up standards for "dash" and "suite."

For *dash* I picture someone running. You could also use a cooking ingredient (a dash of dis, a dash of dat). My standard for *suite* happens to be *sugar.* Surprise, surprise! You could also use honey, molasses, maple syrup, etc. Now, since we know that Ideal Gifts makes gift baskets, picture one of those in your mind's eye. You might see a wicker basket filled with fruits, nuts, candy and other surprises. Or you might simply picture the basket by itself. 208 we will need to break up into the Mental Hooks *nose* (20) and *foe* (8). If I could think of one word or word picture that would fit 208, I would use that, but it really doesn't matter. For the dash, just picture someone running or dashing away. For 4, use the Mental Hook *row*. For U.S. Highway, a gigantic American Flag on a highway filled with *toes* (1) will meet our needs. And for suite, sugar will work. And finally, for the suite number, which is 42, the Mental Hook is *rain*. Let's put it all together in a Chain Link story. Beginning with a basket, the first association is with *nose* (20). See yourself delivering a gift basket to somebody by carrying it on your nose. You might want to picture your nose being much longer than it really is. Maybe even like Pinocchio's. All of a sudden, your worst foe (8) comes along and knocks it off your nose. You are furious at your foe and want to retaliate. Unfortunately, your foe is a lot faster than you and dashes (—) away. And to where does your foe dash?

To the gigantic row (4) in the garden. In that row, your foe finds his/her car and drives away, spotting in the distance the gigantic American flag on the highway (U.S Highway). Heading towards the highway, your foe notices that the highway is filled with thousands and thousands of toes (1). Your foe is amazed when noticing that each of these toes is drinking a spoonful of sugar (suite). Now it begins to rain (42) real hard. Afraid that all of that rain will melt the sugar, imagine yourself taking out a gigantic umbrella in order to protect the sugar from the rain. Congratulations, you have just saved the day! Now go over that entire scenario several times, really making it a point to see each and every one of those associations, and you will have put to memory what for most people would be an extremely difficult address.

Today is the big day. You are being interviewed on television station WFLX T.V. — Channel 29. The studios are at 4119 West Blue Heron Boulevard. For WFLX T.V. — Channel 29, picture a gigantic television set with two huge, muscular arms that are in a state of flex (FLeX). To picture 29, use the Mental Hook *nap*. You can put that into your mental picture by imagining that even though this television set's arms are in a state of flex, it is also in the middle of a nap (29). 4119 is broken up into the Mental Hooks *rat* (41) and *tub* (19). For west, you can picture a *pest* or *vest*, and for Blue Heron, which is a bird, just picture a bird. Even if you don't know what a blue heron bird looks like (I don't), just picturing a bird will probably remind you of the true name. If not, use your imagination and come up with a stronger Soundalike. Now to our Chain Link. We already have our television set, whose muscular arms are in a state of flex (WFLX) taking a nap (Channel 29). See that sleeping, muscle-brained T.V. set scared out of its transistors by a rat (41).

Our heroic boob tube is so frightened it runs as fast as it can without even looking and accidentally trips and falls into a bathtub (19) filled with water. While in the tub, the T.V. set feels a mosquito being a pest (west) and slaps it away. Feeling relieved, our set begins to relax when all of a sudden a gigantic blue heron (blue heron) flies in and scares it again. Once again, run through that scenario several times and you will have it locked.

See How You Do

As a review, fill in the lines below. I am giving you the individual and company names. Beginning with the name, try to remember each association or link in the chain. Assuming you know your Mental Hooks (or have them by your side), you should be able to remember the numbers. When you recall the Soundalikes for street names, as well as the various standards, the true words and names should also come to you. As is the case with everything else in this system, it will work backwards as well as forwards. If you want, briefly go through each of the examples we just did. Then do your best to get as many correct as possible. But most of all, have fun with it, and don't expect to be perfect your first, or for that matter, any time.

Tom Rogers _____

Dave Marconi _____

Thornapple Chevrolet _____

Atlantic Action Limousine _____

Joanne Butler _____

Dial Page_____

Ideal Gifts _____

WFLX T.V. — Channel 29 _____

Check back through the different addresses and see how you did. If you are a bit disappointed, I will almost guarantee that you didn't take the necessary time to really see and lock in those associations. No sweat. If you will go over these addresses one more time and quiz yourself again, you will do better. It is slow at first. The standard shift theory we discussed in the Names and Faces chapter comes into play just as much right now.

Practice For Real-World Application

Finally, a very worthwhile exercise that will allow you to lock in and remember those addresses you need to have in your memory, while providing you with an opportunity to practice. Take out the business cards of the people whose addresses you most need to know from memory. Learn their addresses the same way you learned those in this chapter. And keep those business cards handy. You will want to practice locking in their telephone numbers too, which you will be able to do after you finish the next chapter.

Remember Telephone Numbers

While not in itself likely to make you a millionaire, knowing how to remember telephone numbers is another skill that will undoubtedly prove valuable.

It is said that the genius Dr. Albert Einstein did not know even his own telephone number. When asked why not he replied, and I paraphrase, "I refuse to put something to memory that I can just as easily write down." And Dr. Einstein had a very valid point. However, what about those times when we don't have writing materials while we are hearing what could be a very important telephone number? Or the countless other occasions when knowing a telephone number proves so much more helpful than not knowing it? And imagine how sharp we look when asking a prospect for his/her telephone number, and not bothering to write it down because we are putting it to memory. Talk about effect!

Have you ever dialed Directory Assistance for a telephone number, listened to the computer voice tell you the number, but you didn't write it down? You simply repeated it out loud several times while you dialed the number. Then, to your horror, the line was busy, and you didn't know the number anymore. Did you have to waste valuable time and money calling back Directory Assistance to get the number again? If that has never happened to you before, fine. I'm glad. But if so, then let's rescue you from "411 amnesia." You *can* lock in that number.

This goal is accomplished in much the same way as with addresses, only with a slight difference. The variation is that we are going to make much more use of our knowledge of the Mnemonic Alphabet in order to cut out one extra association as many times as possible. For instance, as you know, the prefix of a telephone number comprises three digits, as do area codes. Now, we could break those into one double-digit Mental Hook and one single, and link the two of them together. Then we would go on to the last four numbers made up, of course, of two double-digit Mental Hooks.

But Let's Make It Even Easier

Why not instead, whenever convenient, make up one word or mental picture for the three-digit prefix. (as well as area codes, but we will get to that later). For example, the prefix 382 could be divided into the hooks *Ma* (38) and *Noah* (2). Or better yet, we could simply see a muffin. The *muh, fuh,* and *nuh* sounds would definitely represent 382, wouldn't they? The prefix 842 could be pictured as a fern. Why? Because we have the *fuh, ruh,* and *nuh* sounds.

The reason we use this procedure is to save a step, but you don't have to. In fact, sometimes it would be impractical to try when there isn't a word that fits the three digits of a particular prefix. Believe me, for the prefix 889, I would break it up into *fife* (88) and *boy* (9). If you can think of a word picture for 889, by all means go for it, and then let me know.

Of course, if you use your imagination enough, you can find a way to do anything. All telephone calling areas use certain prefixes, which you probably call quite often. If you make up a word picture for those prefixes and use them, they will become standards and serve you successfully as do the 100 Mental Hooks you have already put to memory. Incidentally, if you make a lot of long distance calls, you can use the same method to easily remember the various area codes.

Let's begin again with Tom Rogers. Although I used Tom Rogers in the address section, I want to use him also in this section. The reason: to demonstrate that these associations can be used to lock in as much information about somebody as you desire. And that the various pieces of information will not override and overlap each other. Tom Rogers' telephone number is 584-0227. For this we first need to be able to picture the name. Then we have to come up with a mental picture for the numbers 584, and then two Mental Hooks for the last four numbers, 02 and 27. For Rogers, let's again use "Mr. Rogers." For 584, the mental picture of *liver,* the *luh, vuh,* and *ruh* (liver), would definitely be a good representative of 584. The last four digits of the number translate into *sun* (02) and *nook* (27). How about this? Let's picture Mr. Rogers lecturing the children on why they should eat and enjoy liver. Doesn't that almost make sense? You can see Mr. Rogers doing that, can't you? However, this particular liver has been spoiled by the sun (02). There was too much sunlight and it rotted the liver. So see the children taking the liver into their kitchen nook (27) and throwing it out. Review this sequence several times, really seeing each association. Tom Rogers' telephone number is 584-0227.

Let me point out one more time that for the prefix 584, instead of using liver you could use *leaf* for 58 and *row* for 4, and then simply associate Mr. Rogers with a leaf and then a row. Then, of course, you would continue the Chain Link with *sun* and *nook*. You could do it that way, if you choose. I am just trying to save you the extra step.

The next telephone number you need to remember belongs to your accountant, Bruce Strauss; it is 215-5332. In beginning your Chain Link, you could use an adding machine to remind you that this number is for your accountant. In this case, however, he is also a friend, so you want to lock in his number by way of his name. The name Strauss itself does not present a mental picture, does it? Let's use the Soundalike *mouse.* That sounds enough like Strauss to remind you of his true name, doesn't it? For the prefix 215, you can use *noodle* (*nuh, duh* and *luh*). Of course, you could also use *natal, needle* or anything else that would fit, but since I'm suggesting the associations, let's use noodle. The next step is to remember the last four numbers, *lime* (53) and *moon* (32). Now, associate mouse with noodle. See this mouse sneaking his way into a bowl of noodles. In fact, there is one noodle that looks particularly good. You feel the mouse needs to add something to make the noodle taste even better. That's right, some lime (53). See this mouse squirting a sour-tasting lime on that noodle. Now, wanting true dining atmosphere, our squeaky hero goes outside, taking with him this noodle sprayed with lime so he can eat it under the moon (32) light. Bruce Strauss' telephone number is 215-5332.

Your good friend Karen Parks' telephone number is 233-5211. The name Parks does represent something. Simply picture a bunch of parks, whether they are amusement parks or state parks or whatever else *parks* brings to mind. For 233 we have to use our imagination in order to come up with a word picture. How about *name 'em*? Name what? Well, let's look at the rest of the numbers first. 5211 is represented by the Mental Hooks *lion* (52) and *toad* (11). So we have *parks* for Parks, *name 'em* for 233, and *lion* and *toad* for 5211. Let's put them together. In your mind's eye, simply envision many parks. You have been given the right to name 'em (233). As you look over these parks trying to name 'em, you see a big, ferocious lion (52) running by as fast as he can. Why? Because this lion is being chased by a gigantic green toad (11). See that picture in your mind's eye. You are looking over these parks trying to name 'em, when all of a sudden a big, ferocious lion comes running by, chased by a gigantic green toad. Karen Parks' telephone number is 233-5211.

Maybe This One's A Prospect

Let's lock in a business telephone number. You will see that, as is the case with addresses, there basically is no difference between locking in a personal and a business number. For the business number, simply find a mental picture to match the particular industry instead of a person's last name. To illustrate, let's say the number for Abundant Energy, an installer of solar energy systems, is 744-5421. The mental picture you might use for abundant energy is the sun, shaking all over, displaying an abundant amount of energy. For the prefix 744, I use *career*, as the consonant sounds *cuh, ruh* and *ruh* are representative of 744.

The last four numbers, 5421, break up into the Mental Hooks *lawyer* (54) and *nut* (21). In your mind's eye, you can picture the sun displaying all that abundant energy. Why? Because he has a whole career depending upon how much energy he can produce. In fact, the sun is so nervous that he has retained a lawyer (54). Unfortunately, this particular lawyer is really a nut (21). Review the story several times. The telephone number for Abundant Energy is 744-5421.

Next we have the First National Bank. Their telephone number is 744-6285. I'm using the same prefix as the last example to show that it doesn't matter how many times you use it, it will virtually always work. For First National Bank, simply picture a bank. Of course, if you are dealing with various banks and must distinguish this one from the others, simply find a way to put First National into your picture. For example, you might picture this bank having thousands of gigantic blue ribbons hanging from its walls. For 744, you can again use *career*. The number 6285 breaks down into the Mental Hooks *chain* (62) and *file* (85). The bankers I know would probably tell you that to be successful in the banking business you must be totally dedicated to your career. Sometimes, however, the business can be so tough, it feels as though you are wearing heavy chains (62). So what are you going to do? See yourself taking a nail file (85) and filing off that chain. The telephone number for First National Bank is 744-6285.

Could Remembering This Number Save A Life?

Now we come to County Hospital, whose number you would certainly want to know in the event of an emergency. That telephone number is 627-1410. For County Hospital, picturing a hospital should do the trick. For the prefix 627, how about *junk,* which includes the *juh, nuh* and *kuh* sounds? The number 1410 breaks up into *tree* (14) and *ties* (10). Picture a whole group of doctors and nurses emptying the hospital's trash cans of all their junk (627). For some reason, they are emptying this junk into a gigantic tree (14). Not very environmentally conscious of them, is it? And if that isn't bad enough, there are thousands of brand new ties (10) growing off those trees, and now they are ruined from all that junk. Review that weird scenario several times and, in case you ever need the number for County Hospital, you will know it is 627-1410.

Let's put to memory the phone number of radio station WNGS. They call themselves Lite-92, which you also want to remember. Their telephone number is 844-6343. Why don't we just lock it all in? First, the letters WNGS. If you use your imagination, they resemble the word *wings*. So picture some very large flying wings, carrying a radio. The radio has bright light bulbs sticking out. That will remind you of the word *lite*. Sticking way out of one of those light bulbs, however, is a gigantic bone (92). Our scenario up to this point gives us WNGS Lite-92. For the prefix 844, you can use the word *furrier*, as in *more furry*. The number 6343 breaks up into the Mental Hooks *jam* (63) and *room* (43). First, associate wings with furrier. Imagine that it is so cold up where those wings are flying that you reach out and put more fur on those wings. Now those wings are *furrier* (844). The reason why the fur is able to stay on the wings is because you stuck it on using a whole bottle of jam (63). That is somewhat gross, but you will remember it. Now see those wings, which are furrier because you stuck them on with jam, flying right inside your room (43). Again, review the Chain Link. Those wings are carrying a radio with light bulbs sticking out of them. One of those light bulbs, however, is a bone. The wings are furrier because you covered them with fur. You stuck the fur on the wings with a whole bottle of jam, and those wings flew into your room. You just locked in a fair number of facts about that radio station. That is going to take a bit longer than it would have for a shorter Chain Link, but again, I ask you to imagine how long it would take if you didn't have this system.

We Must Get Together

And finally, the telephone number to reach the President at the White House. After all, you might want to invite him and the first lady to dinner next week. The number is (202) 456-1414. To begin the Chain Link, the area code 202 could be represented by *Anacin*™, *Niacin*, *Nissan*™ or anything else that would correspond with those numbers in the Mnemonic Alphabet. Let's use the aspirin *Anacin*™. The prefix 456 could easily be *relish*. And the numbers 1414 are *tree* (14) and *tree* (14). Here is my suggested Chain Link.

It's easy to envision the President having a headache after a bad day of listening to all the world's problems. So he takes two Anacin™ tablets. Make believe that the President dislikes the taste of aspirin so much that he will have it only with relish (456). And we thought jelly beans were funny! This relish is a special Presidential relish that happens to grow on two trees growing in the front lawn of the White House. Now that is one strange story I have just made up. But it works for me, and that is what counts. What is more important is that the stories you make up work for you. Whether you used my story or yours to put to memory the President's telephone number, please go over it in your mind's eye several times. Now you will be able to have them to your home for dinner any time you like. I hope you won't hold it against me if I don't guarantee that last statement.

Again, Put Yourself To The Test

Let's repeat the address exercise we used in the previous chapter as
a review, and fill in the lines below with the correct phone numbers.
Again, I have given you the individual or business names.
Beginning with the name, try to remember each association or link
in the chain. Assuming you know the Mental Hooks (which I hope
you do), or even have them by your side to refer to, you should be
able to recall the numbers. And you know that this will work
backwards as well as forwards. So if somebody takes down a
person's number as part of a message, but forgets to write down the
name, you will be able to recall the name by associating it with the
telephone number.

I would suggest that you go through each of the examples we just
did, making sure to see each association clearly. Then see how you
do.

Tom Rogers	__ __ __ - __ __ __ __
Bruce Strauss	__ __ __ - __ __ __ __
Karen Parks	__ __ __ - __ __ __ __
Abundant Energy	__ __ __ - __ __ __ __
First National Bank	__ __ __ - __ __ __ __
County Medical Center	__ __ __ - __ __ __ __
WNGS Radio Lite-92	__ __ __ - __ __ __ __
The President	(__ __ __) __ __ __ - __ __ __ __

Check back through the various telephone numbers and see how
you did. I hope you did well enough to feel good about it. If you got
fewer correct than you expected, go over those again, really making
it a point to see each association. Then try them one more time to
see how you do. Don't worry, I won't remind you again about
driving a standard shift car. Or did I?

More Real-World Application

I would suggest you also practice this technique with the business cards of people whose numbers you most need to commit to memory. That should prove to be both fun and practical.

In the meantime, just for fun, I am going to give you some area codes for different parts of the country. I will supply the geographic location, its Soundalike, if one is needed, and the area code. You can practice your association skills by making up your own associations between the area and the area code. I won't even suggest pictures for the three-digit numbers.

New York (apple)—212   Los Angeles (angels)—213
Atlanta (Atlantic)—404   Chicago (shy cargo)—312
Philadelphia (philly)—215   Nevada (casino)—702
Utah (you tall)—801   Orlando (oar land doe)—407
Springfield, MA—413   Sweetwater—903
Topeka (toe peek)—913   Toronto (tore a toe)—416
New Orleans (oar leans)—504   Arkansas (I can saw)—501
Rhode Island—401   Wyoming (why a mink?)—307
Omaha (home ha)—402   Orange—714

I can't resist...

212—knittin'	213—knight him	404—razor
312—mitten	215—noodle	702—kissin'
801—fist	407—risk	413—razz 'em
903—best	913—bottom	416—radish
504—laser	501—list	401—wrist
307—mask	402—raisin	714—gutter

Remember Speeches And Sales Presentations

The other day, my dad handed me one of those "surprising facts" columns he took out of our area newspaper. It listed the five situations people fear the most in life. At the top of the list was giving a public speech. That's right! Above death, mice, heights, and yes, even above being forced to sit alone in a room watching endless reruns of "The Misadventures of Sheriff Lobo"!

There are many reasons for this fear of public speaking, including, but certainly not limited to, fear of failure, embarrassment, tensing up, making a fool of oneself, and not being able to *remember* what to say once at the podium.

Why Not Just Write It Down?

You might ask, "Well, what about having the speech written on paper right in front of me so I can simply read it?" The answer to that question is twofold. First, many people are not good public readers. Second, a speech that is read is generally not as well received as one that isn't read. That's because when you don't refer to notes it's perceived you truly know the information. Not to mention the fact that people naturally have a limited attention span. If a speech or presentation is being primarily read word-for-word, with little or no eye contact, that is just how it will come across to that audience. That can make for a very tired, bored audience.

Incidentally, I am not knocking those fears. We all have fears. However, fear of speaking in public is one that can definitely be overcome, and you can have fun while doing it.

Get A Good Start

I often hear people tell me they are totally comfortable talking before one or several people, but just cannot, for the life of them, make themselves speak before a large audience. The funny thing is, after learning how it is done and putting the given suggestions and acquired techniques to work, these same people speak in public before a larger group and they excel.

Back To Basics

As usual, we are going to make effective use of our Mental Hooks, the Chain Link, and Soundalikes. At this point, I need to make clear that this chapter will be taught with the assumption that whenever you agree to give a speech or presentation, you already have ample knowledge of the subject about which you will speak.

Because you are knowledgeable about the subject, or will be by the time you finish your research, you won't have to memorize the speech word-for-word. Simply idea-by-idea, or thought-by-thought. You see, a speech or presentation is simply the detailed explanation of key ideas or thoughts. Assuming you know your subject, if you can remember the key thought at its proper time, your natural memory will help you detail that information to your audience.

To relate an example from personal experience, I often give what are known as keynote, banquet, or after-dinner speeches. They typically run from thirty to sixty minutes in length. These speeches are not intended to teach this entire memory system, since we know it takes longer than that to truly learn it. The speeches are more humorous and entertaining in nature. Combining an overview of the system with several exciting demonstrations of memory skills, I show my audience that improving one's memory can be accomplished by virtually everyone.

I use basically the same format for every presentation, making adjustments in consideration of time, and, believe me, I don't use notes. Wouldn't that look funny? A guy standing there talking about the effectiveness of a trained memory, reading his speech. Or even referring to notes. It could certainly hurt the ol' credibility factor, couldn't it? I give these presentations quite frequently, and by now the entire speech is a permanent part of me. As the saying goes, I could probably do it in my sleep. However, when I was first doing it, I needed to keep a mental outline of what I was going to say.

The presentation consists of six key thoughts or ideas. They are as follows:

1. **Opening** (Acknowledging the group, "It's a pleasure to be here," etc...)

2. **Remembering Names** (This is where I ask everyone in the audience I met earlier for the very first time to please stand up. I then go around the room and, as I individually call back their names, they sit down. Not a bad way to warm up an audience.)

3. **Observation, Association and Imagination** (Why they are so vital to a trained memory.)

4. **Card Counting** (Fun and entertaining. You will learn how to do this in Chapter 18.)

5. **Questions and Answers**

6. **Thank You** (Covers my closing remarks and acknowledgment of the audience for having been so receptive.)

Even back when I first started giving this speech, I was knowledgeable enough of my subject and material to know that if I could remember the key thoughts, then I could explain them in more detail to my audience. Remembering the key thoughts for a presentation such as this could be done in either of two ways.

Link The Key Thoughts...

You could use the Chain Link method and simply link the six key thoughts together. For instance, you would begin the chain by associating *yourself* with *Opening*. You might see yourself opening a door. (You already know how to make the associations imaginative.) Then associate *Opening* with *Remembering Names*. Next associate *Remembering Names* with *Observation, Association and Imagination*. You would next link that concept to "playing cards," for Card Counting. After that would be the association of "playing cards" with *Questions and Answers*. And finally, linking *Questions and Answers* with *Thank You* would give you the last key thought in your speech. Of course, as always, if any of the key thoughts are not tangible, you have to make them tangible in your mind's eye.

...Or Use The Mental Hooks

The second way of accomplishing the same goal would to use the Mental Hooks, which happens to be my personal preference. For example, I did it like this:

1. (Toe) **Opening**—I pictured walking up to the microphone, which wasn't working, and having to use my toe in order to open, or turn it on.

2. (Noah) **Remembering Names**—I imagined Noah asking all the animals on his ark that he had just met for the very first time to please stand up so he could call back their names.

3. (Ma) **Observation, Association and Imagination**—I simply pictured myself explaining to my ma why those three concepts are so important. Picturing my ma observing the speech would also have worked.

4. (Row) **Card Counting**—I pictured myself planting a huge row filled with thousands of playing cards.

5. (Law) **Questions and Answers**—I just imagined my law officer having to answer all sorts of questions.

6. (Chow) **Thank You**—I pictured myself giving thanks for having great chow.

Fairly easy, isn't it? Also, as you know, after doing that presentation several times, the hooks and associations were no longer needed. The speech became true memory. You can bet that putting a speech to memory in this manner and not having to refer to notes makes the communication process appear a lot more natural to your audience. And that makes it easier to be convincing.

Now A Bit More Involved

The next speech we will be putting to memory is a bit more complicated. Many key thoughts will have sub-thoughts and pertinent facts that will also have to be put to memory. This is where it will be necessary to use both the Mental Hooks and the Chain Link, and of course, whenever necessary, the Soundalike.

Let's use a sample speech and lock it in together. It goes without saying that you won't be motivated to really learn and memorize the contents, unless you plan to give that same speech. It will, however, still provide you with the technique, and that's what's important.

The following is an abridged version of a speech given by Toastmaster Dolores McCarthy. It was such a great speech pointing out the positive impact of the elderly in Palm Beach County, Florida, I wish there were room to include the entire text.

Old Means Gold

For years, the nation's older consumer has been ignored or stereotyped as the little old lady shouting, "Where's the beef?" That has changed. In Palm Beach County, old means gold. Old means a better life for you and me. Our standard of living is improving due to the retirees of this county.

After much research, the findings were amazing. Only 3% of all people move after retirement, and only half of them leave the county in which they retired. The ones who do move however, are more affluent, healthier, and have lived a better lifestyle than those who don't. They have more money to spend than the less mobile retirees.

A Palm Beach Post survey reports that the average income of retirees in Palm Beach County is $15,625—25% higher than the state average of $12,147. It has been estimated that from 1975 through 1980, 70,000 older couples moved from New York to Florida. Florida gained about one billion dollars from older migrants at the expense of New York.

Retirees put their money into local banks, fueling loans to local industry. They invest in area real estate, invigorating the construction trade. They shop in local stores, improving retail stability—and they play golf. 40% of all golf courses built in the United States over the past ten years have been built in Florida.

Older Americans spend so many dollars in the state that the Florida Department of Commerce considers the retirement industry as the state's third largest source of revenue.

Of late, people have begun to realize some of these facts; however, I do not think that is enough. We—you and I—have to realize what is happening and we have to take some responsibility for making the retiree feel welcome here. We must realize the positive impact retirees have on our lives. I would ask you next time you shop to be a little friendlier to the elderly. And next time someone old with New York car tags cuts in front of you, just honk your horn and smile or wave. And remember, old means gold, and a better lifestyle for us all.

A smile or a friendly gesture to the elderly may be priceless.

Put It In Writing (Or Typing)

The first thing I suggest when preparing a speech is to write or type it in full. We'll make believe that this was your speech, and that you wrote it with the intention of presenting it. Read completely through your text one time to make sure that what you have written is what you want to say.

Once you have done that and are satisfied with its content, go through it again, this time writing down each key thought. Please notice how I have done that. To remind you of the key thought, write one or even several words. You will also want to note the sub-thoughts.

At this point, I put my key thoughts and sub-thoughts into outline form. You may have used an outline when first putting your ideas together for the text of your speech. That's fine. What I am talking about here, however, is the outline you will use to put your thoughts and sub-thoughts to memory. In other words, your mental outline.

My outline would read as follows:

Old Means Gold

1.   Ignored or stereotyped
     little old lady, "Where's the beef?"
     old means gold
     standard of living improving

2. Research
   3% move after retirement—half leaving county
       in which retired
   affluent, healthier, better lifestyle
   more money to spend

3. Palm Beach Post survey
   average income $15,625
   25% higher than state average $12,147
   estimate from 75-80, 70,000 couples moved from NY to FL
   Florida gained 1 billion dollars at expense of NY

4. Retirees put money into local banks
   local industry
   real estate
   construction trade
   shop locally
   golf—40% of all golf courses built in U.S. in last 10 years
       built in FL

5. Spend so many $$, they are 3rd largest source of state
       revenue

6. Must make elderly feel welcome
   shopping
   cutting off with car
   old means gold

7. A smile or friendly gesture to elderly may be priceless

Seem Familiar?

As you can see, the key thoughts are to be associated with their appropriate Mental Hooks. Once you have put to memory that particular key thought (that which you already know) you will associate it with its first sub-thought (that which you want to remember). From there, you will continue through to the last link in the chain. During your actual speech, when you get to that last link, you will know it is time to go on to the following Mental Hook for your next key thought.

Looking back at the outline, you know what we used as the key thoughts. Let's look at some examples of putting it all together. The first key thought is "ignored or stereotyped." Our first Mental Hook is *toe*. Let's associate toe with ignored or stereotyped. Even though that may seem somewhat difficult, it really isn't. Simply see your big toe being *ignored* by all the other toes. They are ignoring that toe because they have *stereotyped* it as a "typical" big toe, whatever that means.

Our second key thought is "research." The second Mental Hook is *Noah*. In associating those two, one idea might be imagining that Noah did intense *research* concerning the background of every single animal on his ark before departing.

Key thought number three is a "Palm Beach Post survey." The Palm Beach Post is a local newspaper. Our third Mental Hook is *ma*. Let's associate ma with the Palm Beach Post, simply by seeing in your mind's eye your ma sitting down at the breakfast table drinking coffee and reading the *Palm Beach Post*.

The fourth key thought is "retirees put money in local banks." Our fourth Mental Hook is *row*. In order to associate those two concepts, let's use our imagination. In your mind's eye, see a long row of *local banks*. Now see all these retirees approaching this row of local banks in order to deposit their money. Simple as that.

Moving on, our fifth key thought is that retirees "spend so many dollars, they are the state's third largest source of revenue." The fifth Mental Hook is *law,* or police officer. In your mind's eye, picture these senior citizens paying this police officer lots and lots of *dollars* for added protection. That should remind you of the key thought.

The next key thought is that we "must make the elderly feel welcome." Our sixth Mental Hook, of course, is *chow*. That association is an easy one, isn't it? Just invite them to join you for chow. That should make them feel very *welcome*. Remember to make it imaginative.

And finally, the seventh key thought is "a smile or friendly gesture to the elderly may be priceless." The seventh Mental Hook being *cow,* we must associate the two. You could see in your mind's eye a cow walking over to an *elderly* person, and giving that person a big smile. To that *elderly* person, the *smile* was priceless.

All right, we're through setting up our key thoughts. If you are wondering why a couple of them seemed a bit difficult, the answer is that since you didn't write or research the material yourself, you don't know it as well as the author and original presenter. Speeches and presentations will always be easier to put to memory when they are your material. Nonetheless, it can still be done a lot more easily this way than without using the system at all. Let's take, for example, thought number three, the *Palm Beach Post* survey. The author reads that paper daily, thus she would easily make that association with *ma.* In order to remember the name of that paper, you might need to somehow put *Palm Beach Post* into the association. You might see your ma reading a newspaper under a palm tree, or in Palm Beach, surrounded by a fence post.

Link The Key Sub-Points

As you know, even though associating the key thought with a Mental Hook will remind you of that entire idea, there may be specific points concerning your key thought that you feel you definitely need to have committed to memory. We will now form the link from the key thought you now know to sub-thoughts you want to remember.

Going back to our first key thought, which is "ignored or stereotyped," you want to remind yourself that you are going to associate that thought with the little old lady from the food commercial who asked, "Where's the beef?" In your mind's eye you might see your toe, which has been ignored and stereotyped, asking, "Where's the beef?" and your toe begins to eat a hamburger. Crazy picture, isn't it? The next link in the chain is the phrase "old means gold." You might picture that hamburger getting real old and turning into a golden hamburger. Fine. The next sub-point was "standard of living improving." Just say to yourself, "If every hamburger I ever had turned into gold, my standard of living would certainly improve." Fine, now go over those associations several times and you will know your key thought and sub-thoughts.

We know that our second key thought is "research." The sub-point we wish to remember is that "3% move after retirement, only half leaving the county in which they retired." Let's associate those two thoughts. See your *ma,* which represents 3%, doing research on all those people. She is surprised to find that only half actually leave the county in which they retired. Now that we know that sub-thought, we need to link it with "affluent, healthier, better lifestyle." You might imagine your ma feeling happy for those who did leave, as she knows that they are affluent, healthier, and have lived a better lifestyle. Picture them spending their money because they have "more money to spend" and your chain will be complete for your second key thought.

Keep Right On Going

Let's move on to our third key thought: the results of a survey taken by the *Palm Beach Post.* Our first sub-point is the "average income is $15,625." You can handle this in one of two ways. If you can get away with saying "Over fifteen and a half thousand," then simply, in your mind's eye, wrap that newspaper in a *towel,* which, of course, will represent 15. If you need the exact number, 15, 625, no problem. 15 will still be represented by *towel.* Then use your knowledge of the Mnemonic Alphabet to come up with a word picture that includes the six, two, and five. How about channel? Now see yourself taking that newspaper wrapped in a towel, and trying to change the television channel because you're not happy with your income. If you couldn't come up with a word picture, you could still have used the Mental Hooks *chain* and *law,* for 62 and 5.

The next sub-point is that their "average income is 25% higher than the state average of $12,147." How about this? Picture a gigantic *nail* coming out of that television set. The Mental Hook *nail* will represent 25%. You wrap that nail in *tin* foil for 12, and throw it into a *truck,* which could only represent 147.

The next sub-thought is the estimate that "from 1975—1980, 70,000 couples moved from New York to Florida." In your mind's eye, see all those nails wrapped in tin in the truck turning to *coal,* which is 75. And each piece of coal has its own individual *face.* That would stand for 80. Your natural memory will know that 75-80 really represents the years 1975-1980. And each of those pieces of coal with its own individual face was carrying a suitcase, on its way down to Florida. *Case,* the Mental Hook for 70, will remind you that 70,000 couples emigrated from New York to Florida. In case you need to be reminded of the states New York and Florida, you can imagine those suitcases being packed with big apples (NY) and oranges (Florida). In fact, why not imagine those suitcases containing *billions* of big apples and oranges and you will remind yourself of the final sub-point, which is "Florida gained 1 billion dollars at the expense of New York." Review that entire chain once or twice, making sure you *see* those associations.

Don't Sweat It—You're Doing Fine

If at this point you are beginning to feel a bit overwhelmed, please don't. First of all, you probably would not have needed to lock in all those facts and numbers. Also, once you run through that Chain Link several times—assuming the motivation to put the speech to memory is there—you will find the facts and numbers quickly sinking into your true, natural memory.

Our fourth key thought is "retirees put their money into local banks." Let's link on the sub-thoughts. Watch how easy this can be. See that money going to "local industry." Because of all the local industry there are more people who buy houses, which is "real estate." Of course, many of them would like to construct their own homes, which keys your natural memory to the sub-thought "construction trade." Now see all those construction workers getting off work and "shopping locally." Then they go to play "golf." But instead of hitting golf balls, they hit roses, which will remind you that 40% of the golf courses built in the United States over the past ten years have been built in Florida. Go over that entire sequence just a few times, and you will have it. Remember to bend, twist, shake and manipulate this system any way you must, in order to make it work for you.

Since the fifth key thought did not have any sub-thoughts, we can move on to the sixth key point, which is "we must make the elderly feel welcome." The first sub-point is "shopping," so in your mind's eye see a huge welcome sign at the shopping center. The next sub-point deals with the elderly "cutting you off with their car." Link shopping with car by imagining a retiree driving his or her car throughout the shopping center. I mean right through the individual stores! Next sub-thought is "old means gold," so as the car crashes through the building, see the building turning into gold. Again, just run through that sequence several times.

A Great Presentation Still Demands Practice

Finally, the seventh key thought also has no sub-thoughts, so we are done with our mental outline. What you would then do, again assuming you were actually going to give this speech, is practice giving the speech over and over again, working a little more from memory each time. As with everything else we have done thus far, putting speeches and sales presentations to memory gets easier the more you do it. I need to add right here that knowing how to lock in the key ideas of a speech or presentation doesn't mean you won't have to practice, drill and rehearse the speech plenty of times before giving it. Any great performance is preceded by practice. It simply means that it will take you much less time to remember it than it would without the system, and you will know your material much better.

Try The Following

What I would suggest you do as an exercise is to come up with two short speeches of your own. One simple one, that allows you to associate Mental Hooks with key thoughts. And then one where you have some sub-thoughts to link together. Good luck! Take this information to heart, use it, and you will definitely become a more effective speaker.

*C*HAPTER 15

Remember Important Dates

"Youth is the time for adventures of the body, but age for the triumph of the mind."

Logan Pearsall Smith

There's an old saying that the best way for a man to remember his anniversary is to forget it...just once. Fortunately, remembering important dates is much easier than that, and hopefully a lot less traumatic.

Remembering appointments, birthdays, anniversaries, or actually any date can be very important. And after you learn the hooks for the twelve months of the year and the seven days of the week, it will be yet another weapon in your memory arsenal.

It Certainly Couldn't "Hoit"

The benefits of being able to lock in and remember appointments, birthdays or anniversaries may be somewhat obvious, but at the same time you may be asking, "Why should I have to commit information like that to memory? I mean, really Burg, if I've made an appointment for three months from now, believe me, I'm going to write it down in my appointment book."

My answer to that is by all means, write it down. That's one reason why we have pencil and paper. But, as is the case with telephone numbers and addresses, there will be times when having that important appointment or event committed to memory will come in handy.

Assume you are asked by a prospective client to meet on a particular day and time five or six months from now. Even though your appointment book doesn't go that far into the future, you have it locked in your memory. Because of that you can say, "Yes, I'm free that day." Or, "I am already booked with an appointment that morning, but I'm free all afternoon." Might that be somewhat impressive to your future client?

Months Have Their Own Simple Hooks

First, let's learn the Mental Hooks for each month. By and large, the only time you will need to lock in a month will be for remembering someone's birthday or anniversary.

The reason we give each month a Mental Hook is that, as we've experienced throughout this book, it is easier to remember something when it is tangible. Basically, the names of the various months don't present a picture. So let's give each of them pictures we can easily see and remember. Notice the relationship between the months and their hooks.

January—Snow	February—Valentine	March—Marching band
April—Showers	May—Maypole	June—Wedding
July—Jewels	August—A gust (wind)	September—Scepter
October—Witch	November—Turkey	December—Santa

It is important to come up with relevant pictures that can easily be associated with the months they are to represent. Review these a couple of times and I believe you will know them flawlessly, or at least enough to work with effectively. Let's check out a few examples of how these can be put into play.

For both anniversaries and birthdays you will usually know the person or persons involved. So instead of using a Soundalike and associating that with the month and day, you can make the associations by simply picturing the people actually involved. Of course, you can use a Soundalike whenever you want.

Try A Few Examples

For instance, let's imagine that your friend Jennifer's birthday is on January 11. Just associate Jennifer with *snow,* which tells you the month is January, and then link a *toad* onto the picture. Since toad is our Mental Hook representing 11, you will remember that Jennifer's birthday is on January 11. You don't need me to make the associations for you, but please remember to make them as imaginative as possible. You know by now to review that sequence several times, and it will be yours forever.

As I have often done throughout this book, I just want to remind you again that motivation has a lot to do with your ability to lock in and remember new information. I doubt you will remember that Jennifer's birthday is on January 11. That is because you don't need to. There is not sufficient motivation for you to lock in the birth date of someone you don't know. However, when you are locking this information into your mental filing cabinet for real, you will find it really works.

Let's try another example. Make believe your father's birthday is on September 25. Associate your father with a *scepter* and then link onto that picture a *nail,* which is the Mental Hook for 25. It's as easy as that.

Uncle George and Aunt Martha's anniversary is on November 20. Putting that date to memory is easy if you will just associate the two of them with, first, a *turkey* and then a *nose,* for 20.

Your boss's birthday is on March 14. Somehow associate your boss with a *marching band.* And you know what to do next, don't you? That's right. Add a *tree* onto the picture, and you have the date of your boss's birthday put to memory.

One more anniversary: that of your clients. It's their 50th, and you want to be sure and remember because you are going to do something special for that particular one. The date is August 30. Associate your clients with a *gust* of wind, to remind you of August, and then link on a *mouse* for 30. You've got it!

Try Some You Might Be Motivated To Remember

In the blanks below, put to memory some dates of birthdays and anniversaries of people you actually know. First, write down the name of the person or persons involved, along with the date in question; then the appropriate Mental Hook for the month; and finally, the hook for the actual date. Incidentally, if you can more easily remember the subject whose occasion you are trying to lock in by using a Soundalike for his/her name instead of simply picturing that particular person, then by all means go ahead and do so.

Pat Towner-Jan 24	Pat Towner	Snow	Nero
_____	_____	____	____
_____	_____	____	____
_____	_____	____	____
_____	_____	____	____
_____	_____	____	____

Isn't it amazing how truly easy it is to lock in certain information that for most people seems impossible? That's one of the benefits I love about this system. Once you see just how many areas of your life that involve memory can be improved by using these simple techniques (even if it took a bit of practice to perfect), you will realize what an advantage you will have. It won't be long before people ask you how you can remember so much. And being the nice person you are, you will of course personally teach them the system.

Then you will know that you added something very positive to another person's life.

Days Of The Week Also Have Simple Hooks

Now let's look at some Mental Hooks for the days of the week. There will be many times you will have to commit to memory the day of the week you need to be at a particular appointment, your kid's ball game, a concert, or countless other important events. The hooks I use for the days of the week are as follows:

Monday —— Moon

Wednesday — Wedding

Friday ——— Frying pan

Sunday —— Ice cream sundae

Tuesday —— Tweezers

Thursday —— Thirsty

Saturday —— Sat all day

I am sure you noticed the relationship existing in either sound or picture between the days and their hooks. You also may have observed that the hook for Wednesday (Wedding) is the same as the hook for June. Will you ever get confused and mix up the two? You know you won't, because your natural memory will take the situation in its true context and set you straight.

Anybody Happen To Have The Time?

Before we go on to examples, let's first talk about how to plug an appointment *time* into the picture. You can accomplish that by using the Mental Hooks with which you are already familiar. For instance, 1:00 would be represented by your *toe*, 2:00 by *Noah*, 3:00 by your *ma,* and so on until 12:00.

How would you know whether it is a.m. or p.m.? Well, let me ask you this. Would your chiropractic appointment be at 3:00 p.m. or 3:00 a.m.? And if it was an emergency that had to be taken care of at that same time in the morning, all you would need to remember is the 3:00 part of it. You would know the rest.

What about your luncheon appointment? 12:30 a.m. or 12:30 p.m.? See what I mean? You will usually just know. But what about those rare occasions when it could be one or the other? Just have a standard for a.m.: maybe "egg." When remembering the Chain Link later on, if there is an egg at the end of the chain, then you will know your appointment was for the morning. If there is nothing there, you will know it was for the afternoon or evening.

For uneven times, just use your hooks and/or Mnemonic Alphabet as they are needed. For 9:15, you could see your *boy* and a *towel,* or simply a <u>bottle</u>. For 1:45, *toe* and *rail* would work; or you could use <u>Troll</u>.

Have Some Fun With These

Now, let's work with some practice examples. The Chain Link will get a bit more involved, but after a couple of reviews you will know it. Remember, it will still take a lot less time to put to memory than it would without using the system at all.

Let's pretend you have just confirmed an appointment to make a sales presentation to the Board of Directors of Sentry Glass Company. Since this meeting is several months away, you have to be sure not to schedule something else into that time frame without thinking. So you decide to lock in everything, including the month. Sure, you will have the appointment written down in your handy appointment book. What happens though, if soon afterwards someone asks if you are free on that exact day, around the same time, and you don't happen to have your book on you? The situation might result in a lot of unnecessary rescheduling or perhaps even worse—lost business!

Back to our example. Begin with the link on the chain that you already know, Sentry Glass Company. That will, first of all, tell you what it is you are remembering. It is also, however, the first link in the chain of information. Since this is a bit more drawn out than simply remembering someone's birthday or anniversary, I will go through the entire process for this chain, and suggest ideas for the associations.

First, you might picture a sentry guarding a huge piece of glass. That will key off the Sentry Glass Company. Next, let's put in the month, which is May. For May, I use a *maypole.* See the sentry holding that huge piece of glass in one hand as he slides down the maypole with the other. To lock in the date, which is the sixteenth, you might picture your *teacher,* the Mental Hook for 16, scolding him for clowning around by sliding down the maypole. Next, the time of the appointment, 2:30. See the teacher grabbing the sentry's ear and dragging him over to *Noah*'s Ark. That will take care of 2:00. To add in the 30, see them all being chased by a gigantic *mouse.* (Had you wanted, you could have just used the picture of *gnomes* to tell you that the time was 2:30.) To remember that this is to take place on a Monday, just see the entire scenario taking place under the *moon.*

Use Only What You Need

Review that entire series several times and you will own it. This is especially true for a genuine appointment, when the motivation to remember is truly there. Actually, you probably wouldn't even have had to include half the information you locked in, if you were doing it for real. My suggestion is simply link as much information as you feel is needed in order of importance. After the heading, I would usually go with the month, date, time, and finally the day. You might use a different order, which is fine. I would suggest, however, that you stay with the same order every time. It isn't a vital point; your natural memory will usually tell you what was what, but it will help.

In my hometown we have a very nice dinner theatre. They often have great shows. Whenever I have tickets, I mark the date on my calendar, but I also lock it in my mind. I would hate to mistakenly schedule another event for that same date and time.

You Bet Your Life!

For this example, let's pretend that we have tickets to see the play *Groucho, a Life in Review*, which is about Groucho Marx. It will take place on Saturday evening, August 6, beginning with dinner at 7:30.

First we need to picture something to remind us of the play we are going to see: probably obvious in this case. For the remainder of this exercise I will ask you to make the specific associations yourself, while I walk you through the pattern.

Associate your picture representing the title of the play with a *gust* of wind, our Soundalike for August. Onto that link *chow,* the Mental Hook for 6. Next would be a *cow* for 7 and then a *mouse* for 30 (or you could have pictured a bunch of <u>gums</u> for 7:30). Somewhere in that picture, work in *sat all day*, and you will easily remember that the play is on Saturday.

You Wouldn't Want To Miss This

Let's try another example. In fact, an even more important theatrical event, your daughter's school play, is this month on the twenty-fifth. She is playing one of the cute little munchkins in *The Wizard Of Oz.* The play falls on a Friday evening and you need to be there by 6:00 in order to help set up.

First, lock in the event you want to remember by picturing something that will serve as a reminder of the play's title. That should be easy enough. The month doesn't need to be consciously locked in since you know it is this month. Associate your picture representing *The Wizard Of Oz* with a *nail,* which is the Mental Hook for 25. Now you know the date. Onto that, link *chow,* which, of course, is the Mental Hook for 6, in this case representing 6:00. Finally, put a *frying pan* into that picture to remind you that the play is on a Friday evening.

How about just one more example? You are a Realtor®, and you have a closing that is scheduled to take place on Tuesday, April 12 at 3:00. The seller's last name is Olson. Begin with the mental picture that for you represents the name Olson. Take the picture you now have for Olson and associate it with *shower,* which represents the month of April. Next, link onto that some *tin,* or tin foil, which will tell you that the closing date is the twelfth. Onto that, link your *ma,* for 3:00. Finally, if you want to remember that April 12 will fall on a Tuesday, you can throw a pair of *tweezers* into the picture.

Anything else you feel you might need to lock into that picture is simply added as another link onto the chain. For instance, to lock in the place where the closing is to take place, let's say your office, which is Memory Realty, just add a picture to remind you of the name; possibly a finger with a string tied around it. Or maybe a light bulb over a head, or whatever. Now run through that chain several times and you will remember it.

A Very Worthwhile Skill To Own

Yes, it takes a few moments of conscious effort, but it's worth it. You will soon discover that the security you'll feel will definitely outweigh the relatively small amount of effort. I suggest you review the examples we just did, and then in the spaces provided, come up with a few of your own. Remember, practice makes just about perfect.

Practice
Practice
Practice
Practice
Practice
Practice

Event	Month	Date	Time	Day
_____	_____	_____	_____	_____
_____	_____	_____	_____	_____
_____	_____	_____	_____	_____
_____	_____	_____	_____	_____
_____	_____	_____	_____	_____
_____	_____	_____	_____	_____
_____	_____	_____	_____	_____
_____	_____	_____	_____	_____

Remember What You Read

In today's fast paced society, we are surrounded by information. Whether the medium is newspaper, national magazine, trade publication, or even an instruction manual, the ability to remember information after a single reading can be another valuable skill on the road to your success.

Speed reading is fine to know, and there are many excellent courses offered on the subject. However, mastering comprehension, and effectively filing away the information to be recalled when needed, is the focus of this chapter, not necessarily speed. Of course, when you can remember the desired information after one read-through, you will in essence be increasing your speed as well.

Not A Trick

Have you ever heard about people who can read an entire issue of a magazine, and hours later, when asked what is on a certain page, be able to answer correctly? Or, when they are given some of the information on a particular page, they can come up with the correct page number? You can do that, too! All you need to know for that impressive demonstration of memory are the Mental Hooks. (The really nice thing is that it serves a practical purpose as well.)

Let's look at how it is done. Simply take the key idea of a particular page and associate it with its corresponding Mental Hook. For example, if page 1 is the Table of Contents, then associate that with your *toe*. If page 2 is an advertisement for U.S. Sprint, associate it with *Noah*. Yes, it is that simple and of course will also work in reverse.

If you wish to lock in additional facts, simply employ the Chain Link Method. For instance, let's pretend the article on page 79 was entitled "Closing the Sale." First, you would associate closing the sale with a *cup,* the Mental Hook for 79. You might see yourself spilling your cup of coffee all over the table where the closing just took place. Then you would look at the first key point relating to the article, say *providing excellent service*. Just link closing the sale on to the picture you would use for providing excellent service. See yourself hiring a cleaning *service* to clean up the coffee you just spilled. Now, let's make believe that the final important point of the article dealt with "how to get referrals from your new customers." You know to link that onto your story. You might see yourself being so pleased with the cleaning service that you refer them to someone else who has just spilled their coffee, and so on and so on. This can go on indefinitely, until you have covered and put to memory all the desired key points of the article.

Notice How Easy It Really Is

Let's use another example, this time from a fictional magazine called *Sales Training Today*. The following illustration gives the page number and title of each article we will lock into our memory.

Page 6 is entitled "Letters to the Editor." To remember, simply associate the sixth Mental Hook, *chow,* with the key thought *letters.* Possibly see yourself eating from your bowl of chow and taking spoonful after spoonful of gigantic envelopes that contain letters to the editor.

Page 10 has a very interesting article on telephone prospecting techniques. You know that to remember this you must form an association between the tenth Mental Hook, *ties,* and a *telephone.* Imagine your telephone wearing several ties in order to look good during prospecting.

The article on page 18 delves into techniques of successful negotiation. Associating taffy, the eighteenth Mental Hook, with negotiating is easy if you can picture yourself wanting the last piece of *taffy* so desperately that you are willing to *negotiate* for it with someone else. Will the negotiations be successful?

Page 27 pertains to buying a franchise. The twenty-seventh Mental Hook is *nook,* which means you must somehow associate your kitchen nook with *franchise.* Can you imagine yourself buying a franchise, any franchise, and running it right out of your kitchen nook? Talk about low overhead!

On page 34 you noticed a very good article on motivation. Your thirty-fourth Mental Hook is *mower,* therefore associate mower with motivation. Are you the type that must really motivate yourself to get out there and mow your front lawn?

Page 52 had several ads for a cassette tape series. You might want to buy some, so associate *lion,* the fifty-second Mental Hook, with *cassette tape series.* Imagine a lion driving in his car and popping in a cassette tape to listen to and learn from. Now there is a lion who takes advantage of drive time!

On page 60, you noticed an article on time management. The sixtieth Mental Hook is *cheese.* How can we associate cheese with time management? Imagine yourself having only one piece of cheese that has to last you for an indefinite amount of time. Be sure and manage that time well, okay?

"Entrepreneurs of the '90s" is the title of the article on page 73. Associate that concept with the seventy-third Mental Hook, *comb,* in order to remember it. Picture your favorite entrepreneur, like Lee Iacocca, Ted Turner, or Debbie Fields (Mrs. Fields cookies), running a gigantic comb through his or her hair.

On page 86 there is an article on how to choose a chief financial officer for your company. The eighty-sixth Mental Hook is *fish.* Imagine hiring a fish as your company's chief financial officer. See that fish looking the part as much as possible and you will surely be able to remember the association.

The article on page 96 discusses everyday prospecting for business. Since the Mental Hook for 96 is *beach,* see yourself doing your prospecting on the beach. You might not meet many new prospects but will, at the least, get a good tan!

Finally, page 105 has an article on body language as it relates to sales. Let's make use of the Mnemonic Alphabet and for 105 picture a diesel engine truck. Associate the picture of a diesel with *body language* by seeing the diesel truck contorting its body, or you contorting your body, perhaps in an attempt to sell the diesel engine truck on the idea of not running over you.

Are You Impressed With Yourself?...You Should Be!

There you have it. If you know your hooks, you can demonstrate remembering the pages of a book, magazine, or anything else you desire. Or, use these techniques for your personal betterment. And yes, once again, the process works in reverse. You can also link on to the main title, the author's name, and key sub-points you want or need to put to memory. You will find that when you lock in the key points of an article, or just the title, you will actually remember a significantly greater amount of the entire article.

Remember History For School

The information in this chapter relates directly to those still in school; however, the techniques and exercises can be beneficial to anyone. Back in Chapter 10 we learned how to lock in historical facts and dates. This chapter will provide more detail and give you an opportunity to use your memory skills, make up your own associations, and then quiz yourself.

A history teacher at a local high school supplied me with a list of what she felt were important dates in history that anyone in school should know. Most are related to the United States, while some refer to other countries.

In the left-hand column is the date. In parentheses after the date are the appropriate Mental Hooks. Remember, use only those hooks you feel are necessary to effectively lock in the dates. For example, 1858 (taffy, leaf) was the year of the Lincoln-Douglas debates. If you already know the event occurred in the 1800's, then simply associate the Lincoln-Douglas debates with *leaf*; you don't need *taffy* in the association.

The Mental Hooks are followed by the event. The significance of the events will not be explained, since the purpose of this chapter is simply to practice locking in historical dates. Here we go!

1492	(tree, bone)	—	Columbus discovered the new world
1607	(teach, sock)	—	Founding of Jamestown
1620	(teach, nose)	—	Mayflower Compact
1776	(tag, cash)	—	Declaration of Independence
1776-83	(tag, cash, foam)	—	American Revolutionary War
1783	(tag, foam)	—	Treaty of Paris
1787	(tag, fig)	—	Constitutional Convention
1789	(tug, fob)	—	French Revolution
1791	(tag, boat)	—	Bill of Rights
1803	(taffy, sum)	—	Louisiana Purchase
1812	(taffy, tin)	—	War of 1812 (JUST JOKING!)
1820	(taffy, nose)	—	Missouri Compromise
1823	(taffy, name)	—	Monroe Doctrine
1846-48	(taffy, roach, roof)	—	Mexican War
1851	(taffy, light)	—	*Uncle Tom's Cabin* published
1858	(taffy, leaf)	—	Lincoln-Douglas Debates
1861-65	(taffy, chute, jail)	—	American Civil War
1863	(taffy, jam)	—	Emancipation Proclamation
1865	(taffy, jail)	—	President Abraham Lincoln assassinated
1865	(taffy, jail)	—	13th Amendment; abolition of slavery
1876	(taffy, cash)	—	Battle of Little Big Horn
1886	(taffy, fish)	—	Founding of the American Federation of Labor (AFL)
1890	(taffy, base)	—	Sherman Anti-Trust Act
1901	(tub, suit)	—	Assassination of President William McKinley
1914-18	(tub, tree, taffy)	—	World War I
1917	(tub, tag)	—	Russian Revolution, resulting in communist takeover
1919	(tub, tub)	—	Treaty of Versailles
1920	(tub, nose)	—	19th Amendment; Nationwide suffrage given to women
1927	(tub, nook)	—	Lindbergh flight
1929	(tub, nap)	—	Stock market crash
1933	(tub, mummy)	—	The rise of the Third Reich
1939-45	(tub, map, rail)	—	World War II
1947	(tub, rake)	—	Marshall Plan
1948	(tub, roof)	—	Berlin Blockade
1950-53	(tub, lease, lime)	—	Korean War
1962	(tub, chain)	—	Cuban Missile Crisis
1963	(tub, jam)	—	Assassination of President John F. Kennedy
1964	(tub, chair)	—	Gulf of Tonkin; U.S. full involvement in Vietnam
1968	(tub, chief)	—	Assassination of Dr. Martin Luther King, Jr.
1973-74	(tub, comb, core)	—	Watergate scandal
1979	(tub, cup)	—	Camp David Accords
1980	(tub, face)	—	Ronald Reagan elected President of U.S.

I suggest you quiz yourself by either covering up the dates and attempting to match them with the event, or vice versa. You can also ask someone to give you a quiz orally. Or just for fun, see how you do with these examples (you might first want to quickly review them one final time):

Mayflower Compact _____

Lindbergh Flight _____

Cuban Missile Crisis _____

Emancipation Proclamation _____

Watergate scandal _____

Mexican War _____

Treaty of Paris _____

Reagan Presidential Election_____

Lincoln assassination _____

Marshall Plan _____

To lock permanently in your memory the dates of any or all of the 42 events we covered in this chapter, review them several times over the course of two or three days. Before you know it they'll become a part of your long-term memory.

*C*HAPTER 18

Remember Those Playing Cards

Would you like to dramatically increase your odds of winning at card games, including Bridge, Rummy and Blackjack? How about amazing your friends and associates with an incredible demonstration of memory? Or would you be interested in knowing a really great exercise that will allow you to flex the muscles of your mind? If you answered yes to any of these questions, then I invite you to learn the information in this chapter.

At practically every seminar or keynote speech I give, I conclude with a display of card counting that leaves the audience amazed, wondering how it could possibly be done. I make a point to explain beforehand is that it isn't a trick, it is simply a demonstration of a trained memory.

Here's The Demonstration

Let me tell you what I do. I have one person shuffle the cards. Very often I will have another person reshuffle just to assure the Doubting Thomases in the audience that this is not a trick. It soon becomes obvious that I have no idea as to the order of the cards.

Next, someone else randomly draws between 15 and 20 cards from the deck in no particular order. They can, of course, choose more or less than that amount; it doesn't matter at all.

The cards that were not chosen are then given to four volunteers at the front of the room. They are each asked to take a suit. One person takes all the clubs; one the hearts, one the spades, and the last person the diamonds. Again, it doesn't have to be in any particular order. I also ask the volunteers to put the cards in numerical order, with the ace as the low card.

While that is taking place, I turn my head away and ask the person who has drawn the 15 to 20 cards to call them out loud one at a time. As the person does this, I lock them into my mental filing cabinet.

After all the cards have been called, I ask the participant with the clubs to stand before the audience, with the cards fanned out so that everyone can see them clearly. I am the only one in the room who can't.

Then, starting with the ace and moving up to the king of that suit, I tell the audience which cards the person has and which he doesn't. In other words, "In his hands he has the ace of hearts, the two of hearts, he doesn't have the three of hearts, he has the four of hearts, but he doesn't have the five of hearts, he doesn't have the...," until I get to the king. Then it is time for the next suit, and then the next.

What amazes the audience is that through memorizing the cards as they were pulled out of the deck and called aloud, I can tell everyone what cards the volunteers are and are not holding in their hands.

Hooray For Hollywood

Of course, I also throw in a little "gingerbread," or showbiz for good measure. I might wait until the person has announced all the cards to the audience before telling the four volunteers to put the cards in numerical order with the ace as the low card. At that point I'll even begin talking about something else for several minutes. Then I will share with the audience the reason I delayed so long between hearing the cards called out and announcing which cards are and are not in the hands of the volunteers: "Just in case any of you in the audience were trying to remember the cards by rote memory... I'm giving you a chance to forget." I get a laugh every time from that one because half the audience was probably trying to do exactly that. The other half probably thought it was so difficult that they weren't even trying.

Trust me when I say that you too will be able to do this very same exercise, and you'll soon realize just how simple it is. Soooo very simple!

Turning The Intangible...Into The Tangible

Why are playing cards so difficult to remember for most of us? If I compare them to numbers and Zap! Names does that tell you? Sure, because by and large, playing cards are also intangible. After all, they are made of numbers; not to mention four suits of each: clubs, hearts, spades and diamonds. Now add some pictures, an ace, a jack, a queen and a king, again four of each, and you have 52 intangible little items on your hands.

Knowing our memory improvement system as you do, you of course realize that the answer is to turn these intangible items into objects we can see or picture with hooks. Each card will have a hook, a picture we can see and work with effectively. Now, the question remaining is how to come up with 52 individual hooks, without the time it takes to remember them, outweighing the benefits of being able to commit them to memory.

EASY! We'll use our Mnemonic Alphabet, and we'll do it like this: the mental picture, or hook, for each card in the clubs suit will begin with the letter c, as in club. The next consonant sound will correspond to its value in the Mnemonic Alphabet.

The ace, which has the value of one, would be represented by the "t" or "d". Therefore, for the ace of clubs, you could picture a *cat*. You could also picture a *coat* or *cot* or *cod*. Of course, we will only need to choose one, and then stay with it. The two of clubs could easily be represented by a *can, cane, cone*, or more. Pick one and stay with it. The nine of clubs would begin with *c* and end with the sound corresponding to the nine. *Cap* would work; so would *cab, cop* and a myriad of other items.

The Others Simply Follow "Suit"

The other suits would work the same way. The three of hearts would begin with the letter *h* and end with the "muh" sound. It could therefore be represented by *ham, hem,* and *home,* among others. The two of spades would have to begin with the letter *s* and end with the "nuh" sound. *Son* or *sun* are two appropriate representations that come to mind. The six of diamonds would begin with *d* and end with a sound representative of 6 in the Mnemonic Alphabet. How about *dish,* or even *dash,* for which you might picture someone running?

Before I list some of the many choices you have for playing card hooks, let me show you how I handle hooks for the face cards. There are actually two ways to do this. One would be to follow the same pattern and see the jack as being the numerical equivalent of 11, the queen as 12, and the king as 13, for which I will list examples. Or, you could do what I do. For the jacks, I simply see a picture of that particular suit. In other words, for the jack of clubs I picture a *club.* The jack of hearts is represented by a heart. Actually, for that card I picture the Tin Man from the *Wizard of Oz.* He's the one who wanted the heart. I picture a *spade,* or shovel, for the jack of spades. Finally, for the jack of diamonds, I picture a *diamond.*

For the queens and kings I simply begin with the letter of the suit and try, for the most part, to make the rest of it rhyme with queen or king . For instance, for the king of diamonds I picture a *drink.* For the king of spades I use *sing,* for which I picture a famous singer. The queen of spades reminds me of *seam,* for which I picture a sewing machine. For the king of clubs I picture a *King.* For the queen of hearts I picture a *Queen.* I personally feel that putting the picture cards to memory like this is easier than using the Mnemonic Alphabet, but do what you feel will work for you. Since this concept varies from our usual method, I won't even list these hooks in the examples below. Aside from the jacks, I will keep them all by Mnemonic Alphabet.

Next to the actual card name there will be a blank space followed by several suggestions. In that blank space please write the word for the picture you are going to use. You can either use one of my suggestions or something totally different. As long as all the hooks (excluding the jacks, and possibly the queens and kings) fit the guidelines dictated by the Mnemonic Alphabet, and are distinct from one another, anything you use will work.

Clubs ♣

AC	_____	(cat, coat, cot)
2C	_____	(can, cane, cone)
3C	_____	(cam, comb)
4C	_____	(car, core)
5C	_____	(coal)
6C	_____	(cash, catch)
7C	_____	(cake, coke)
8C	_____	(calf, cuff)
9C	_____	(cap, cop, cup)
10C	_____	(case, cuz<cousin>)
JC	_____	(club)
QC	_____	(cotton, cuttin')
KC	_____	(Cut 'em<scissors>)

Hearts ♥

AH	_____	(hat, hut)
2H	_____	(hen, hun, honey)
3H	_____	(ham, hem, home)
4H	_____	(hair, hare)
5H	_____	(hail, hall, hole)
6H	_____	(hash, hedge)
7H	_____	(hag, hog, hug)
8H	_____	(hoof, huff)
9H	_____	(hippie, hop, hoop)
10H	_____	(haze, hose)
JH	_____	(heart)
QH	_____	(hittin')
KH	_____	(hate 'em)

Spades ♠

AS	_____	(set, soot, suit)
2S	_____	(son, sun)
3S	_____	(sum <adding machine>)
4S	_____	(sewer, sore)
5S	_____	(sail, sill, sole)
6S	_____	(sash <window>)
7S	_____	(sack, sock)
8S	_____	(safe)
9S	_____	(sap, soap, soup)
10S	_____	(suds)
JS	_____	(spade)
QS	_____	(skiin', satan, satin)
KS	_____	(sick 'em)

Diamonds ♦

AD	_____	(date, dot)
2D	_____	(dane, den, dune)
3D	_____	(dam, dome)
4D	_____	(deer, door)
5D	_____	(Dole™, doll)
6D	_____	(dash, dish)
7D	_____	(deck, dock, duck)
8D	_____	(dive, dove)
9D	_____	(deb, dip)
10D	_____	(dice, dose)
JD	_____	(diamond)
QD	_____	(deadin')
KD	_____	(deed 'em <land>)

Time For A Quick Review

Before going on, I suggest you take a few moments to review these hooks. Go over them once or twice just to familiarize yourself with them, and at some point in the future, drill yourself in order to really know them well. The way I did it was exactly the same way I learned the 100 regular Mental Hooks. I made flash cards.

Whenever there was a spare moment I quizzed myself. If you know your Mnemonic Alphabet (and by now I certainly hope you do) you too should have your playing card hooks down pat very shortly. Let's now use these hooks for the demonstration mentioned earlier. Refer back to the hooks as you feel necessary. We are going to remember which cards were called and which cards remained in the hands of the four volunteers via a method called "mutilation."

For this example, we will make believe the person drawing the cards from the deck took 17 different cards. The only reason I ask the person to take between 15 and 20 cards is due to time limitations. Otherwise it wouldn't matter how many cards were picked.

As each card is called out, we are simply going to mutilate, or at least alter, that card's hook in our mind's eye. Then later, as we run through the cards in each suit, we'll know that the ones not mutilated are in that volunteer's hands. If that sounds difficult, this practice drill will illustrate how simple it really is.

Here Are The Cards

I am now going to write out each of the 17 cards. As you come to each one, please see its hook, or mental picture. Immediately after we finish the list, I will demonstrate how I would mutilate it. You don't have to use my hooks, or mutilate them as I do, but for the purpose of learning how this works, I would suggest that you do. The cards are...6D, 4C, 7H, 10C, 8D, 8H, 2H, JS, 2C, KS, AH, 4S, KS, 3D, 3C, 9H and AS.

Now let's mutilate each picture.

6D	(dish)	—	See a dish breaking into a thousand pieces as it hits the floor.
4C	(core)	—	See yourself mashing an apple core into apple sauce.
7H	(hog)	—	Imagine bacon frying in a pan.
10C	(case)	—	Picture a briefcase opening and all the papers flying out.
8D	(dive)	—	A diver takes a bad fall off the diving board and gets hurt.
8H	(hoof)	—	See a horse being shoed and not liking it one bit.
2H	(honey)	—	Imagine sticky honey all over your hands.
JS	(spade)	—	Picture a spade, or shovel, breaking in two while in the ground.
2C	(cone)	—	See your delicious ice cream cone falling on the ground.
KS	(sic 'em)	—	You tell your dog to sic 'em, but he lies down instead.
AH	(hat)	—	Picture yourself punching a hole right through your hat.
4S	(sore)	—	Imagine the bandage covering your sore shredding to bits.
QS	(skiin')	—	See yourself skiing and taking a big fall.
3D	(dam)	—	The dam breaks and the water goes all over the place.
3C	(comb)	—	Your comb breaks in two as you run it through your hair.
9H	(hoop)	—	As you dunk the ball through the hoop, the backboard shatters.
AS	(suit)	—	Imagine a tear in your brand new suit.

We've thus gone through our 17 cards. Let's now see if we can tell our audience which cards the four volunteers are carrying and which ones they are not. As a piece of advice, I go in the same order every time I do this demonstration: clubs, hearts, spades and diamonds. You don't necessarily have to go in that particular order; however, choosing one set order that you always use will eliminate any confusion you might encounter. In any case, you can always find an easy way of remembering which suits you have done, so you don't *forget* and start doing the same suit over again. However, it will be easier if you use a pattern. And as you can tell, I like to make things as easy for myself (and for you) as possible.

To Have Mutilated, Or Not To Have Mutilated

All we are going to do now is simply run through the deck out loud, beginning with the ace, or one, of a particular suit, and work our way up to the king. While doing this, we will tell the audience what cards the volunteer is holding and what cards he's not. As you run the gamut, you know that if you see that particular card, or hook, being mutilated, then the volunteer doesn't have it. If it isn't mutilated, then the volunteer does have it.

The volunteer holding the clubs now stands in front of the audience, fanning out the cards so that everyone but you can see them. Let's impress our audience.

- The first card you would picture is the AC, for which we pictured a *coat*. Did you somehow, in your mind's eye, mutilate or alter a coat? No, so you know the person has the AC.

- Next is the 2C. Did you mutilate a *cone?* Yes, your ice cream cone fell to the ground. Therefore, you know the volunteer does *not* have the 2C. That would be impossible, since that card had to be called out among the 17 for you to have mutilated it. See how it works?

- Let's move on to the 3C, which is a *comb.* Was it mutilated? Yes, it broke in two when you ran it through your hair, so the person is not holding the 3C.

- Next is the 4C, or *core.* You mashed that apple core into apple sauce, thus, the volunteer does not have the 4C.

- Let's move on to the 5C, which is *coal.* Did you mutilate the coal? No, so the person has it in her hands.

- What about the 6C, which is cash? Was the cash mutilated? No, it wasn't; therefore the person is holding the 6C.

- And the 7C, which is *cake?* Still intact, isn't it? So you know the person is holding the 7C.

- The 8C is *cuff.* Did you somehow mutilate a cuff? No, so the volunteer has the 8C.

- The 9C is *cap.* Mutilated? No, so it is still in the person's hands.

- The 10C is represented by the word *case,* for which a briefcase is pictured. Did you mutilate that briefcase? Yes, you did. Do you recall the briefcase opening and all the papers flying out? Then you know the volunteer does not have the 10C.

- The next card is the JC, for which a *club* is pictured. Did you mutilate a club? No, so the person still has the JC.

- The QC, or *cotton,* comes next. Was it mutilated? No, so the person must still have that QC.

- Finally, the KC, for which we pictured scissors for *cut 'em,* was not mutilated; therefore the volunteer must still be holding that card.

Try The Rest Yourself

Now it is up to you to go through the other three suits in the same way. As you come to each card, you will know that if it wasn't mutilated, the person must still have it. If it was mutilated, then he or she doesn't. This is one fun and impressive demonstration of your trained memory! Of course, it only makes sense that the better you know your cards and their hooks, the faster and more impressive you can be.

Different Forms Of Mutilation

If you find yourself in a position where you must do a number of these demonstrations within a short period of time (say within an hour), don't panic. You will, however, need to find a few different ways to mutilate the hooks. Otherwise, you will have an overlap from one demonstration to the next. So for the second time, mutilate the hooks by lighting them on fire. The third time, maybe spray mace on them. The next time, rip all the pictures apart. Douse them with water the following time. After that, associate them with one of the people in the audience. It's all a matter of how imaginative you can be.

If you plan to do a demonstration once on a given day, and then again a few hours later, no sweat. By that time overlap will no longer be a problem and you can go back to your original mutilations. That sounds sort of sick, doesn't it?

You will probably never be in a situation where you would do the demonstration enough times that you would have to come up with all the different mutilations. But they could all come into play during card games where you need to know which cards have been played, discarded, thrown, etc., and which have not.

Find Practical Applications For These Techniques

I'm certainly not an expert on cards. I don't play often enough to have an understanding of the rules and strategies. Many of my students, however, tell me they have taken this technique and, combined with their knowledge of the various card games, have improved their chances of winning. It's up to you to take these skills and techniques and turn them into a more effective way to play your cards.

You Can Use Your Mental Hooks As Well

Speaking of impressive demonstrations, as well as another good mental exercise, how about this next one? Have a person shuffle and then randomly take the 52 cards, one by one, and call them off in sequence. For instance, "Number one is the four of hearts, number two is the jack of diamonds, number three is the ...," etc. All you do is associate each card with its corresponding Mental Hook. For the first card, the 4H, associate your *hair* with *toe*. The JD, represented by a *diamond,* would be associated with *Noah.* And on and on through the last card called, which you would associate with *lion,* the fifty-second Mental Hook. Then tell that person to call out a number between 1 and 52 and you will call out its corresponding card. Next, ask that person to call out a card and you will say its corresponding number. Neat, isn't it? Of course, it will take less time to do it with 10 or 20 cards, but that is up to you. Now you know how it is done.

But please, I have one favor to ask of you. After you do this demonstration and someone asks how you did this neat *card trick,* please politely set them straight and tell them "it is not a trick, but simply a demonstration of a trained memory."

*C*HAPTER 19

Overcome Absentmindedness

We've all had bouts with absentmindedness. They may have been caused by preoccupation or inattention to our present needs or surroundings. Whatever the circumstances, we didn't think about what we were doing while we were doing it. How to decrease the occurrence of absentmindedness in everyday life will be the focus of this chapter.

Let's Explore The Two Kinds

There are basically two types of absentmindedness. One concerns an action we have already done; the other, something we plan to do.

Several cases in point of the first kind: putting away, or temporarily putting down, car keys, eyeglasses, pens, or briefcase. Where? Then there is always the question, "Did I take my medication this morning, or didn't I?" Another popular one is, "Did I turn off the stove before I left the house?"

The second type involves not remembering an idea or a task intended to be done in the very near future. Sometimes, immediately after getting an idea to do something, or even being told to do it, the thought leaves our mind. For example, forgetting to stop at the grocery store for a loaf of bread and milk on the way home from work, or to pick up little Suzie after school. Whoops!

Taking the Steps To Improve

While no one is immune to either type of occasional, temporary losing of the mind, there is a way to dramatically decrease its frequency. You may have already guessed that we will again use our powers of observation, association, and imagination. We observe the action while doing it (or thinking it), associate it with something we already know, and then use our imagination to make the action or thought memorable.

Has This Ever Happened To You?

Let's look at a real-life example to demonstrate how to help overcome the first type of absentmindedness. You put your car keys on the living room coffee table before heading into another room. In order not to forget where you put them, you decide to formally lock in the information. So explode the coffee table. That's right, picture your coffee table exploding as it is touched by the keys. See the keys flying all over the room, as they would have had there been a true explosion. I can almost guarantee that when you reenter the living room and think about your keys, you will remember the explosive action and head right for the coffee table. The same method can be used for glasses, briefcases, or anything else you commonly misplace or temporarily forget the whereabouts of.

Here's a suggestion for remembering to take your morning medication. At the time you take your dosage, imagine that you have just swallowed fire, and see the fire coming out of your mouth, just like in a fire-breathing dragon. Later in the day, when wondering whether or not you took your medication, you'll definitely remember that fire scene. If you have to take your medication three times a day, simply devise another imaginative association for noon and evening. For example, if you use fire for the morning dosage, use ice for noon and ink for evening, whatever picture suits your fancy. If you're going to be on a certain medication for an extended period of time, take the solution a step further. Remember our Soundalikes for the days of the week? Monday-moon, Tuesday-tweezers, Wednesday-wedding, Thursday-thirsty, Friday-frying pan, Saturday-sat all day, and Sunday-ice cream sundae. Therefore, if you took your medication on a Tuesday, associate the action with tweezers; if the day was Friday, with a frying pan. It's all up to you and how imaginative you want to be. If making these associations seems like a lot of work, then I can only assure you that once you get into the habit, it'll be a snap.

A String Around Our Brain

Now let's work on the second type of absentmindedness: the times you know you must do something, but are not sure if you can or will remember to do it. The way we will cover this problem is with a mental string around the finger. We have all seen the illustration of someone tying a string around his/her finger to be reminded of a task. Just having the string will clue your natural memory into remembering what it is you have to do. Let's, however, try another method since wearing a string around your finger is not one of your "cooler" social moves.

Imagine that your spouse calls you at work and asks you to pick up a loaf of bread and a bottle of milk. Take a moment right then to imagine a gigantic loaf of bread, or a bottle of milk, driving your car. When you get into your car at the close of the work day, you will probably remember what you have to do.

What about an idea you might get while you are driving? My suggestion would be to picture in your mind's eye that your car will explode when you take the key out of the ignition, once you get to your destination. When that happens, you will remember the specific idea, at which time you can either do it or write it down. If you feel a physical cue might be even safer, then you could tilt your rear view mirror in such a way that you can't help notice it when you stop your car. That will also trigger your memory. Still another way to physically remind yourself of something is to temporarily wear your wristwatch on your other wrist—also very effective.

Where Did I Park That Car?

Finally, I would be remiss if I did not give you a simple way to remember where you parked your car in a number-letter-coded parking lot. The airport is a perfect example. Have you ever returned from a trip and realized that you could not remember where you had parked your car? Here is a fail-safe way of putting that information to memory, using both Mental Hooks and Alphabet Hooks. If the space where you parked your vehicle was 4B (fourth level, aisle B), simply associate it with a *row* of *bees*. If the space you parked was 7C, then associate your car with a *cow* and the *sea*. It is absolutely as simple as that! In my line of work, I often find myself heading toward the long-term parking garage of my local airport and I haven't missed yet! Of course, the day I do forget, everyone who owns this book will probably be there to witness it.

You will invent your own specific reminders, both mental and physical, as you continue to experiment. The few moments it takes to make the associations will save you hours in the long run, and besides, it's great fun having a memory working for you instead of against you.

*C*HAPTER 20

Apply What You Have Learned

"Memory is the receptacle and sheath of all knowledge."
—Cicero 50 B.C.

Even back during Cicero's time (actually, well before) the importance of a skilled and effective memory was acknowledged. Now you too have discovered and learned a method for implementing these skills and techniques in your life. Whether you decided to learn these skills simply for fun or to increase your earning potential, the rewards are there for you to reap and enjoy.

Unfortunately, many people read a book such as this as if it were a novel—skimming through, finding some of the ideas interesting, but not taking the time to study, go through the exercises, and practice. I can only tell you that if your goal is to master this system, then that is what you must do. I would suggest going back through the book to the topics that are most germane to your personal goals, reread the chapters, and yes, do the exercises. Not every topic will be important to you, and that is okay. As long as you know the basic system, including the Mnemonic Alphabet, Mental Hooks, Chain Link and Soundalikes, you can pursue the specific areas you desire.

I would like to leave you with a saying. It is one of my all-time favorites, and I feel it relates so well to effectively learning this memory system.

PERSISTENCE

Nothing in the world can take the place of persistence.

TALENT WILL NOT

Nothing is more common than unsuccessful people with talent.

GENIUS WILL NOT

Unrewarded genius is almost a proverb.

EDUCATION WILL NOT

The world is full of educated derelicts.

The slogan "Press on" has solved and always will solve the problems of the human race.

—Calvin Coolidge 30th U.S. President

To all of you with the persistence to make things work, I wish you the...

Best of Success..."AND GOOD MEMORIES!"

*I*NDEX

3 concepts of memory, 1,7

6 steps to remembering names, 27,33

absentmindedness:

       2 types of, 191,192

       overcoming, see chapter 19

       steps to improve, 192-194

addresses, remembering, see chapter 12

       advantages of, 133

       examples and exercises, 134-140

       use of celebrities as soundalikes or mental hooks, 134

       using standards, 134,135

alphabet soundalikes and alphabet hooks, see chapter 11

       as mental hooks, 130,131

       chart of, 124

       examples of use, 125-131

Americana, remembering, see chapter 10

       examples of, 115-120

       exercise over, 122

associate something with something, 3

association:

       defined, 2,3

       learning to make, 13

       subconscious, 4

       word association, as memory technique, 5

card counting, 181
Carnegie, Dale, 25
celebrities as soundalikes or mental hooks, 134
Chain Link Method:
    defined, 9
    example of, 9-12
    fundamental to good memory, 9
    purpose of, 9
checking account number, remembering, 90
dates, making tangible, 6
dates, remembering, see chapter 15
    advantages of, 163
    days of the week, 167
    examples, 165,166,168-171
    months, 164
directions, standards for remembering, 134,135
first names, 36-39
flash cards:
    to learn mnemonic alphabet, 86
    with mental hooks, 107
foreign language vocabulary, see chapter 6
foreign languages, need to be fluent in, 73
historical dates, important, list of, 178
history, remembering, see chapter 17
imagination:
    6 methods of, 13-15
    defined, 5
    imaginative associations most effective, 12
    importance of, 5
imagination-association, 6 techniques,
    action, 14
    bizarre, 14
    exaggeration, 14,15
    make yourself the star, 15
    pain, 14
    substitution, 14
imagination skills, developing, 13-15
intangible:
    letters, 123
    names, 26
    numbers, 81,82
    playing cards, 183
    use of soundalike for picturing, 15,16

keynote, banquet or after dinner speeches, 152
letters, are intangible, 123
memorabilia, see chapter 3
  remembering, 21
  use of mnemonic initialing in, 22
memory remedies, 93
memory, definition of, 1
mental hook, see chapter 8
  chart, 94,97
  correspondence to mnemonic alphabet, 97,106
  examples of associations, 102-104
  exercises, 100-105
  explained, 96
  use of flash cards with, 107
  in presentations, 154
mnemonic alphabet, see chapter 7
  correspondence to mental hook, 97
  chart of, 85
  checking account number, 90
  exercise, 87,91
  explained, 83,84
  in counting cards, 184
  social security number, 89
  use of flash cards, 86
  use of for remembering telephone numbers, 144
mnemonic initialing, 22,23
mnemonics, misunderstandings regarding, 3
mutilating playing cards, as memory device, 186-190
names and faces, remembering, see chapter 4
names:
  are intangible, 26
  observing, 28,29
  soundalikes for, list of, 47-61
names, remembering, see chapter 4
  6 steps to, 27,33
  examples of, 31-33,39-42
  with groups, 45
networking, using memory to enhance, 44,45
numbers:
  Arabic, 83
  are intangible, 81,82
  with groups, 45
  checking account, remembering, 90

difficulty in remembering, 81
need to picture, 82
remembering, exercise, 87
remembering via mnemonic alphabet, see chapter 7
serial number of TV set, 125,126
social security, remembering, 89
observation:
always involved in memory, 1-7
begin by, 1,2
importance of observing names, 28
to improve memory, 2
observation, association, imagination, 1-7
always involved in memory, 7
as learned skills, 1-7
essential components of memory, 1
original awareness, 1
outstanding facial feature,
explained, 27
use of in memory, 27,28
examples of, 39-42
playing cards:
are intangible, 183
counting, 181
remembering, see chapter 18
presentations:
demand practice, 162
example, 157-159
put it in writing, 156
outlining, 156,157
presidents, remembering, see chapter 9
list of, 109-113
public speaking, fear of, 151
quick reference:
first name soundalikes, 47
last name soundalikes, 48-61
reading, comprehending and remembering, see chapter 16
serial number of TV set, remembering, 125,126
Social Security numbers, 89
soundalike:
defined, 15,16
in vocabulary, list of examples, 65-71
to picture the intangible, 15,16
use of to improve vocabulary, 64

speeches and sales presentations, remembering, see chapter 14
       example, 155-161
speed reading, 173
standard shift analogy, 36,44
standards for real estate transactions, chart, 127
telephone numbers, remembering, see chapter 13
       business numbers, 146,147
       exercise, 149
times, remembering, 167
trained memory, definition of, 1
vocabulary,
       distinguishes success from mediocrity, 63,64
       importance of a large, 63,64
       improving, 64,65
       improving, examples, 65-71
vocabulary, Foreign, see chapter 6
       French, 76,77
       importance of knowing, 73
       improving knowledge of, examples, 74-79
       Italian, 77,78
       Serbo-Croatian, 78,79
       Spanish, 74-76
wild and crazy pictures, 13
word association, as memory technique, 5
ZAP! Names, 17,29,183

YOUR BACK-OF-THE-BOOK STORE

Because you already know the value of National Press Publications Desktop Handbooks and Business User's Manuals, here's a time-saving way to purchase more career-building resources from our convenient "bookstore."

- IT'S EASY … Just make your selections, then visit us on the Web, mail, call or fax your order. (See back for details.)
- INCREASE YOUR EFFECTIVENESS … Books in these two series have sold more than two million copies and are known as reliable sources of instantly helpful information.
- THEY'RE CONVENIENT TO USE … Each handbook is durable, concise and filled with quality advice that will last you all the way to the boardroom.
- YOUR SATISFACTION IS 100% GUARANTEED. Forever.

60-MINUTE TRAINING SERIES™ HANDBOOKS

TITLE	RETAIL PRICE*	QTY.	TOTAL
8 Steps for Highly Effective Negotiations #424	$14.95		
Assertiveness #4422	$14.95		
Balancing Career and Family #4152	$14.95		
Common Ground #4122	$14.95		
The Essentials of Business Writing #4310	$14.95		
Everyday Parenting Solutions #4862	$14.95		
Exceptional Customer Service #4882	$14.95		
Fear & Anger: Control Your Emotions #4302	$14.95		
Fundamentals of Planning #4301	$14.95		
Getting Things Done #4112	$14.95		
How to Coach an Effective Team #4308	$14.95		
How to De-Junk Your Life #4306	$14.95		
How to Handle Conflict and Confrontation #4952	$14.95		
How to Manage Your Boss #493	$14.95		
How to Supervise People #4102	$14.95		
How to Work With People #4032	$14.95		
Inspire and Motivate: Performance Reviews #4232	$14.95		
Listen Up: Hear What's Really Being Said #4172	$14.95		
Motivation and Goal-Setting #4962	$14.95		
A New Attitude #4432	$14.95		
The New Dynamic Comm. Skills for Women #4309	$14.95		
The Polished Professional #4262	$14.95		
The Power of Innovative Thinking #428	$14.95		
The Power of Self-Managed Teams #4222	$14.95		
Powerful Communication Skills #4132	$14.95		
Present With Confidence #4612	$14.95		
The Secret to Developing Peak Performers #4962	$14.95		
Self-Esteem: The Power to Be Your Best #4642	$14.95		
Shortcuts to Organized Files and Records #4307	$14.95		
The Stress Management Handbook #4842	$14.95		
Supreme Teams: How to Make Teams Work #4303	$14.95		
Thriving on Change #4212	$14.95		
Women and Leadership #4632	$14.95		

MORE FROM OUR BACK-OF-THE-BOOK STORE
Business User's Manuals — Self-Study, Interactive Guide

TITLE	RETAIL PRICE	QTY.	TOTAL
The Assertive Advantage #439	$26.95		
Being OK Just Isn't Enough #5407	$26.95		
Business Letters for Busy People #449	$26.95		
Coping With Difficult People #465	$26.95		
Dealing With Conflict and Anger #5402	$26.95		
Hand-Picked: Finding & Hiring… #5405	$26.95		
High-Impact Presentation and Training Skills #4382	$26.95		
Learn to Listen #446	$26.95		
Lifeplanning #476	$26.95		
The Manager's Role as Coach #456	$26.95		
The Memory System #452	$26.95		
Negaholics® No More #5406	$26.95		
Parenting the Other Chick's Eggs #5404	$26.95		
Taking AIM On Leadership #5401	$26.95		
Prioritize, Organize: Art of Getting It Done 2nd ed. #4532	$26.95		
The Promotable Woman #450	$26.95		
Sex, Laws & Stereotypes #432	$26.95		
Think Like a Manager 3rd ed. #4513	$26.95		
Working Woman's Comm. Survival Guide #5172	$29.95		

SPECIAL OFFER:
Orders over $75 receive
FREE SHIPPING

Subtotal		$
Add 7% Sales Tax		
(Or add appropriate state and local tax)		$
Shipping and Handling		
($3 one item; 50¢ each additional item)		$
Total		$

VOLUME DISCOUNTS AVAILABLE — CALL 1-800-258-7248

Name_____Title_____

Organization _____

Address_____

City _____State/Province _____ZIP/Postal Code _____

Payment choices:

❏ Enclosed is my check/money order payable to National Seminars.

❏ Please charge to: ❏ MasterCard   ❏ VISA   ❏ American Express

Signature _____Exp. Date _____Card Number _____

❏ Purchase Order #_____

MAIL: Complete and mail order form
with payment to:
National Press Publications
P.O. Box 419107
Kansas City, MO 64141-6107

PHONE:
Call toll-free **1-800-258-7248**

INTERNET: www.natsem.com

FAX:
1-913-432-0824